THE UNIVERSE OF THINGS

Cary Wolfe, Series Editor

(continued on page 181)

THE UNIVERSE OF THINGS

On Speculative Realism

STEVEN SHAVIRO

posthumanities 30

University of Minnesota Press

Minneapolis

London

Chapter 1 was previously published as "Self-Enjoyment and Concern: On Whitehead and Levinas," in *Beyond Metaphysics? Explorations in Alfred North Whitehead's Late Thought,* ed. Roland Faber, Brian G. Henning, and Clinton Combs (New York: Rodopi, 2010), 249–58. Chapter 2 was previously published as "The Actual Volcano: Whitehead, Harman, and the Problem of Relations," in *The Speculative Turn: Continental Materialism and Realism,* ed. Levi Bryant, Nick Srnicek, and Graham Harman (Melbourne, Australia: re.press, 2011), 279–90. Chapter 3 was previously published as "The Universe of Things," *Theory and Event* 14, no. 3 (2011).

Published by the University of Minnesota Press
111 Third Avenue South, Suite 290
Minneapolis, MN 55401-2520
http://www.upress.umn.edu

Library of Congress Cataloging-in-Publication Data

Shaviro, Steven.
   The universe of things : on speculative realism / Steven Shaviro.
     (Posthumanities ; 30)
   Includes bibliographical references and index.
   ISBN 978-0-8166-8926-2 (pb : alk. paper) — ISBN 978-0-8166-8924-8 (hc : alk. paper)
   1. Whitehead, Alfred North, 1861–1947. 2. Realism. I. Title.

B1674.W354S435 2014
192—dc23   2013049860

Printed in the United States of America on acid-free paper

The University of Minnesota is an equal-opportunity educator and employer.

20 19 18 17 16 15   10 9 8 7 6 5 4 3 2

THIS BOOK IS DEDICATED TO MY DAUGHTERS,
ADAH MOZELLE SHAVIRO AND ROXANNE TAMAR SHAVIRO.

CONTENTS

ACKNOWLEDGMENTS

It is impossible for me to offer a complete list of people who helped me with the various stages of this project. I would like especially to thank Michael Austin, Jane Bennett, Ian Bogost, Levi Bryant, William Connolly, Roland Faber, Erick Felinto, Mark Fisher, Alexander Galloway, Richard Grusin, Graham Harman, N. Katherine Hayles, Matija Jelača, Timothy Morton, Dominic Pettman, Scott Richmond, Isabelle Stengers, Eugene Thacker, McKenzie Wark, and Ben Woodard, together with others whose names have been inadvertently omitted here.

ABBREVIATIONS

Books by Alfred North Whitehead are cited by the following abbreviations:

AI   *Adventures of Ideas*
CN   *The Concept of Nature*
MT   *Modes of Thought*
PR   *Process and Reality*
RM   *Religion in the Making*
SMW   *Science and the Modern World*
SP   *Science and Philosophy*

INTRODUCTION

Whitehead and Speculative Realism

THIS BOOK TAKES A NEW LOOK at the philosophy of Alfred North Whitehead (1861–1947) in the light of a number of recent developments in continental philosophy that can be grouped under the rubrics of "speculative realism" and (to a lesser extent) "new materialism." I seek to relate the divergent programs and goals of these new strains in philosophical thought both positively and negatively to Whitehead's own project. The biggest reason for looking at the resonances and connections between these two bodies of thought is this: Whitehead and the speculative realists alike question the anthropocentrism that has so long been a key assumption of modern Western rationality. Such a questioning is urgently needed at a time when we face the prospect of ecological catastrophe and when we are forced to recognize that the fate of humanity is deeply intertwined with the fates of all sorts of other entities. Anthropocentrism also has become increasingly untenable in the light of scientific experiment and discovery. Now that we know how similar, and how closely related, we are to all the other living things on this planet, we cannot continue to consider ourselves as unique. And we cannot isolate our own interests, and our own economies, from processes taking place on a cosmic scale in a universe whose boundaries we are unable to grasp.

Alfred North Whitehead was already aware of these tensions and dangers nearly a century ago. The basic aim of Whitehead's philosophy is always to overcome what he called "the bifurcation of nature," or the absolute division between "the nature apprehended in awareness and the nature which is the cause of awareness" (*CN*, 30–31). On the one hand, Whitehead suggests, we have the world's phenomenal appearance to us: "the greenness of the trees, the song of the birds, the warmth of the sun, the hardness of the chairs, and the feel of the velvet" (*CN*, 31). On the other hand, we have the hidden physical reality, "the conjectured system of molecules and electrons which so affects the mind as to produce the awareness of apparent nature" (*CN*, 31). Much of modern thought is founded on this bifurcation, whether it takes the form of an opposition between primary and secondary qualities (Descartes and Locke, revived by Quentin Meillassoux), or between noumena and phenomena (Kant), or between the "manifest image" and the "scientific image" (Wilfrid Sellars and, most recently, Ray Brassier). Phenomenology, and continental thought more generally, sits on one side of this bifurcation; the more scientistic and reductionist versions of analytic thought sit on the other side. But Whitehead seeks to do away with the bifurcation altogether. "We may not pick and choose," he says; we must develop an account of the world in which "the red glow of the sunset" and "the molecules and electric waves" of sunlight refracting into the earth's atmosphere have the same ontological status (*CN*, 29).

Whitehead's quest to overcome the bifurcation of nature led him into a long course of metaphysical speculation. His final, developed philosophy, expressed in his magnum opus *Process and Reality* (1929) and further refined in his final books *Adventures of Ideas* (1933) and *Modes of Thought* (1938), articulates a vision of cosmological scope. The world, he says, is composed of processes, not things. Nothing is given in advance; everything must first become what it is: "*how* an actual entity *becomes* constitutes *what* that actual entity *is* . . . Its 'being' is constituted by its 'becoming'" (*PR*, 23). Understood in this way, the process encompasses both sides of the bifurcation of nature: it applies equally to what I apprehend and to the manner in which I apprehend it. I am not a subject confronting (or "intending," as the phenomenologists would say) an object-world that lies outside of me, for both "subject" and "object" are themselves processes of becoming, and "all actual things are alike objects [and] subjects" (*PR*, 56–57).

Most Western philosophy since Descartes, and especially since Kant, has reinforced the bifurcation of nature because it is centered on questions of cognition. It privileges epistemology (which asks the question of *how* we can know what we know) at the expense of ontology (which directly poses the question of what is). The Cartesian cogito, the Kantian transcendental deduction, and the phenomenological epoche all make the world dependent on our knowledge of it. They all subordinate *what is known* to our *way of knowing*. But Whitehead, to the contrary, insists that "things experienced are to be distinguished from our knowledge of them. So far as there is dependence, the *things* pave the way for the *cognition*, rather than *vice versa* . . . the actual things experienced enter into a common world which transcends knowledge, though it includes knowledge" (*SMW*, 88–89). That is to say, the question of *how we know* cannot come first, for our way of knowing is itself a consequence, or a product, of how things actually are and what they do. Epistemology must be deprivileged, because we cannot subordinate things themselves to our experiences of them. I do not come to know a world of things outside myself. Rather, I discover—which is to say, I *feel*—that I myself, together with things that go beyond my knowledge of them, are all alike inhabitants of a "common world."

What is crucial in Whitehead's account is that each particle of being— each "actual entity" or "actual occasion" or process of becoming— transcends all the rest; yet, at the same time, all these "occasions" belong together. Whitehead thus proposes a double view of the world. On the one hand, "the ultimate metaphysical truth is atomism" (*PR*, 35); each entity is different, and separate, from all the others. But on the other hand, these ultimate atoms are "drops of experience, complex and interdependent" (*PR*, 18). That is to say, they are active and articulated processes— experiences, or moments of feeling—rather than simple, self-identical substances. In this way, being is subordinated to becoming; yet becoming is not an uninterrupted, universal flux, but a multiplicity of discrete "occasions," each of which is limited, determinate, and finite (*PR*, 35 and passim). Whitehead thus affirms both the deep interrelatedness of all things and the ways that their interactions and variations continually lead to consequences that are new and unforeseen. Whitehead's highest value is *creativity*, which he calls "the universal of universals" (*PR*, 21). This means that the world is never static, never closed, never completed. Each process of becoming gives rise to *novelty*: it produces something new and unique, something that has never existed before. Things do not "persist in being" (the definition of Spinoza's *conatus*) so much as they continually alter and transform themselves, exhibiting "a certain originality . . . originality of response to stimulus" (*PR*, 104).

Whitehead died in 1947. His philosophy went into eclipse during the second half of the twentieth century—a time when the very endeavor of what he called "speculative philosophy" (*PR*, 3–17) was regarded with scorn. Whitehead's work was largely ignored by analytic and continental philosophers alike and taken up only by a small group of "process theologians" (see, e.g., Cobb and Griffin 1976). Today, however, in the early twenty-first century, there has been something of a revival of interest in Whitehead's thought. This is largely due to the publication of major studies of Whitehead by Judith Jones (1988) and by Isabelle Stengers (2011); my own previous book on Whitehead, *Without Criteria: Kant, Whitehead, Deleuze, and Aesthetics*, follows in their footsteps (Shaviro 2009). The recent revival of interest in Whitehead has also been spurred by an increasing recognition of the affinities between Whitehead's process-oriented thought and that of the French philosopher Gilles Deleuze.

But more generally, Whitehead has become newly relevant due to a changed climate of thought. Although he was born in the Victorian age and did his major work at the time of early modernism, Whitehead seems uniquely relevant to our current postmodern (and posteverything) era of digitization and globalization. He returns to haunt us at a time when, after having passed through a century of relentless modernist attempts at formalization and purification, we begin to realize that perhaps "we have never been modern" in the first place (Latour 1993). Today, we live in an age characterized by digital sampling, ecological crises, and the emergence of the posthuman. Whitehead is deeply relevant to our contemporary concerns because he thinks about how novelty can emerge from selective repetition, how all the entities of the world are deeply interrelated and mutually dependent even in their separation from one another, and how nonhuman agents, no less than human ones, perform actions and express needs and values.

It is within this context that I locate the convergence between Whitehead's concerns and those of the speculative realists and new materialists. The name "speculative realism" was first introduced in 2007 to describe the work of four philosophers: Quentin Meillassoux, Graham Harman, Ray Brassier, and Iain Hamilton Grant. Other thinkers who might be added to the group include Levi Bryant, Ian Bogost, Timothy Morton, Eugene Thacker, and Ben Woodard. All these thinkers in fact disagree strongly among themselves, as well as with Whitehead, on a number of fundamental issues (for a survey of speculative realism in its various modes, see Bryant, Srnicek, and Harman 2010). But they are united—as the name indicates—by a common commitment, shared with Whitehead, to metaphysical speculation and to a robust ontological realism. They all seek to restore the dignity of metaphysical investigation and invention after a century in which any sort of "metaphysics" was almost phobically rejected. And like Whitehead, these recent thinkers are all forthright realists—in contrast to the way that so much twentieth-century thought was premised on a fundamental antirealism. As Lee Braver demonstrates in detail, phenomenology, structuralism, and most subsequent schools of twentieth-century continental philosophy assume one version or another of the antirealist, Kantian claim that "phenomena depend upon the mind to exist" (Braver 2007, 39 and passim). It is this assumption, above all, that speculative realism seeks to overturn.

More precisely, the speculative realists are united by their rejection of what Meillassoux calls *correlationism*. This is the doctrine according to which "we never grasp an object 'in itself,' in isolation from its relation to the subject" (Meillassoux 2008, 5). For correlationism, a mind-independent reality cannot exist, because the very fact that we are thinking of such a reality means that it is not mind-independent after all. From this point of view, "thought cannot get *outside itself* in order to compare the world as it is 'in itself' to the world as it is 'for us', and thereby distinguish what is a function of our relation to the world from what belongs to the world alone" (Meillassoux 2008, 3). In correlationism, as Brassier puts it, "since it is impossible to separate the subjective from the objective, or the human from the nonhuman, it makes no sense to ask what anything is in itself, independently of our relating to it" (in Bryant et al. 2010, 53–54). Or in the words of Harman, under correlationism, "everything is reduced to a question of human access to the world, and nonhuman relations are abandoned to the natural sciences" (2009b, 156). In other words, Harman continues, "the correlationist holds that we cannot think of humans without world, nor world without humans, but only of a primal rapport or correlation between the two. For the correlationist, it is impossible to speak of a world that pre-existed humans *in itself*, but only of a world pre-existing humans *for humans*" (2009b, 122). As Harman sarcastically summarizes the position, correlationism assumes that "what is thought is thereby converted entirely into thought, and that what lies outside thought must always remain unthinkable" (2010, 789).

The speculative realists are keenly aware that the self-reflexivity of the correlationist argument—the way that it reflects back critically on its own premises—makes it difficult to escape. Once we find ourselves within what Meillassoux calls "the correlationist circle" (2008, 5), we cannot easily step outside of it again. The seemingly self-confirming self-evidence of the correlationist circle has dominated Western philosophy for nearly two and a half centuries. Correlationism goes back at least to Kant's "Copernican revolution" in philosophy, according to which our very experience of the world can take place only under conditions of our own making. The correlationist argument is not empirical, but what Kant calls *transcendental*: it provides us with the very *conditions* that govern our understanding and our discourse. That is to say, correlationism is not so much explicitly argued for as it is always already preassumed by both sides in any post-Kantian philosophical debate. With his transcendental argument, Kant refutes all forms of "dogmatism" (metaphysical attempts to describe what the world is actually like, in and of itself), together with what today is commonly disparaged as "naïve realism." Such positions are impossible, Kant says; because we do not have access to "things in themselves," we cannot know anything about them—aside from the sheer fact that they must exist. Kant's transcendental argument is designed to ensure that, in the words of Meillassoux, "one cannot think the in-itself without entering into a vicious circle, thereby immediately contradicting oneself" (2008, 5).

In the wake of Kant, correlationism continued to dominate Western philosophical discourse throughout the nineteenth century and well into the twentieth. We find correlationist assumptions both in phenomenology, with its concept of a fundamental noetic-noematic structure, and in the early work of Wittgenstein, with his argument that "the metaphysical subject" is "the limit of the world—not a part of it" (Wittgenstein 1922/2001, sec. 5.641). Later in the century, deconstruction remains at least negatively correlationist when it claims that there is no outside-the-text (*il ny'a pas de hors-texte*; Derrida 1998, 158), no realm of being entirely outside, or independent of, the infinite play of language or textuality. And Lacanian psychoanalysis also fails to make enough of a break with correlationism. Indeed, it posits a Real that cannot be correlated with thought. But it presents this Real as being radically undifferentiated so that—precisely like the Kantian thing-in-itself—it is "*thoroughly non-substantial* . . . a product of failed attempts to integrate it into the Symbolic" (Žižek 1993, 129). Here the subject–object correlation is negated, but for that very reason, the Real is still not posited outside of the correlationist horizon. Even the radical poststructuralist thought of the late twentieth century remains enslaved to what Harman calls "the bland default metaphysics that reduces objects to our human access to them" (2009b, 25).

Whitehead anticipates the speculative realist critique of correlationism, although of course he never uses that word. His own explicit objection is to what he calls the "subject–predicate forms of thought" and the accompanying "'substance–quality' concept" that have dominated the history of Western philosophy since Aristotle (*PR*, 7). Under the subject–predicate schema, Whitehead says, "there is no perception of a particular actual entity," but only a series of generalizations, or "characterizations by universals" (*PR*, 49). We never truly encounter things outside of ourselves; this ultimately leads to Kant's "degradation of the world into 'mere appearance'" (*PR*, 49). We are trapped within the bifurcation of nature when we divide the world into actual, material things that are inaccessible to us, on the one hand, and the impressions or ideas of these things that subsist in the mind, on the other. Against this tradition, Whitehead insists that we actually do directly encounter things other than ourselves: "an actual entity *is* present in other actual entities" (*PR*, 50). Things are never just passive or inert; they have *powers*, by virtue of which they are able to affect things other than themselves (*PR*, 57–59). Things move us, or force us to feel them, and by this very fact they elude the correlational schemas in which we would wish to contain them.

Whitehead also anticipates speculative realism in that, for him, "Man" is not the measure of all things. He is one of those rare philosophers who, as Harman rightly says, dares to venture beyond the human sphere (2005, 190). Becoming and creativity are "generic notions" for Whitehead (*PR*, 17, 18); they do not refer to human beings in particular but apply to all happenings in the cosmos. There are, of course, differences of degree; as Whitehead several times reminds us, for instance, a human being exhibits a greater amount of originality than does a stone (*PR*, 15, 104). But these differences of degree are never converted into differences of kind. Even a stone is ultimately active and transformative; it cannot just be regarded as an instance of "quiet undifferentiated endurance" in which certain fixed qualities would inhere (*PR*, 77–79). In appreciating the powers and sufficiencies even of a stone, Whitehead steers Western philosophy away from its inveterate anthropocentrism. He proposes a metaphysics that instead accords the same ontological status to "throbs of pulsation, molecules, stones, lives of plants, lives of animals, lives of men" (*MT*, 86).

Meillassoux suggests that, trapped in the correlationist circle, "contemporary philosophers have lost the *great outdoors*, the *absolute* outside of pre-critical thinkers; that outside which was not relative to us . . . existing in itself regardless of whether we are thinking of it or not; that outside which thought could explore with the legitimate feeling of being on foreign territory—of being entirely elsewhere" (2008, 7). Whitehead never aimed to offer a critique of correlationism. And yet he anticipates many of the themes and arguments of speculative realism. This is because he already moves in the element of the great outdoors—by means of what Stengers calls his "free and wild creation of concepts" (2011). And this is why, just as Meillassoux reverts to Descartes in order to sidestep the correlationist circle, Whitehead, despite his unavoidably post-Kantian frame of reference (as I have discussed at length in Shaviro 2009), explicitly announces that his work involves "a recurrence to that phase of philosophic thought which began with Descartes and ended with Hume" (PR, xi).

The only way to outfox correlationism, and reach the great outdoors, without simply falling back into what Kant rejected as "dogmatism" is to proceed obliquely through the history of philosophy, finding its points of divergence and its strange detours, when it moves beyond its own anthropocentric assumptions. The aim is not to critically document the closures and omissions of traditional metaphysics, as did Heidegger and Derrida. Indeed, both Heidegger and Derrida are far more Kantian than either of them would have cared to acknowledge; their work radicalizes and completes the Kantian project of turning reason back on itself in order to expose its own unavoidable illusions. In contrast to this, both Whitehead and Meillassoux seize on the contradictions and hesitations of classical philosophy, not as points of critical intervention, but as tools for regaining the great outdoors. That is to say, they reach toward those anomalous moments when classical philosophy offers radical formulations that contradict and exceed its own "tacit presupposition[s]" (PR, 76).

Speculative realism is not without its dangers. In seeking to break out of the correlationist circle, it takes a risk: "the move toward realism is not a move toward the stuffy limitations of common sense, but quite often a turn toward the downright bizarre" (Bryant et al. 2010, 7). Even if breaking away from "stuffy . . . common sense" is admirable, it can also bespeak a contemptuous arrogance, implicitly suggesting that "everyone else is deluded, but I know better." Whitehead warns us that "there is a constant reaction between specialism and common sense" (*PR*, 17); it will not do simply to throw out the latter, even when we are seeking to alter it. Also, affirming the bizarre for its own sake, in order to shock others, is an old modernist trick that has become boring and tedious at this late date. At its worst, speculative philosophy is a lot like speculative finance, leveraging vast amounts of credit (both fiscal and metaphysical) on the basis of shaky, dubious foundations (or no foundations at all). But at its best, speculative philosophy rather resembles speculative fiction, for it cannot do without extrapolation. Speculative philosophy works, as Whitehead puts it, through "the complex process of generalizing from particular topics, of imaginatively schematizing the generalizations, and finally by renewed comparison of the imagined scheme with the direct experience to which it should apply" (*PR*, 16). The same might well be said of science fiction, and indeed, the line between science fiction and speculative metaphysics is often quite difficult to draw.

The speculative realists are united by their rejection of correlationism and their commitment to "a speculative wager on the possible returns from a renewed attention to reality itself" (Bryant et al. 2010, 3). But they differ radically from one another, as well as from Whitehead, in their positive programs of metaphysical speculation. Meillassoux argues that mathematics has a unique ability "to discourse about the great outdoors; to discourse about a past where both humanity and life are absent" (2008, 26). Through a kind of inverted transcendental argument, he arrives at an absolute ontological claim for "the necessity of contingency" (71). That is to say, he argues that "contingency *alone* is necessary" (80). Ray Brassier turns less to mathematics itself than to the mathematical formulations of contemporary physical science in order to grasp a material reality that is not correlated with human thought in any way. He seeks to show how "scientific conception tracks the in-itself," or how "science knows reality," without conceptualizing that reality, "without resorting to the Aristotelian equation of reality with substantial form" (in Bryant et al.

2010, 64). Harman, together with his colleagues Levi Bryant, Ian Bogost, and Timothy Morton, elaborates what he calls object-oriented ontology (OOO). This proclaims a "democracy of objects" (Bryant 2011) and works "to place all objects on equal footing" (Harman 2009b, 103), thereby "ceasing to regard the rift between objects and human perception as the sole chasm in the universe" (Harman 2005, 192). Grant, for his part, returns to Schelling's criticisms of Kantian correlationism in order to propose a new "nature philosophy" in which materiality is "*dynamically* conceived as *consisting only* in actions" (Grant 2006, 39) and thought itself is situated as a product of forces that both precede and exceed it (Grant 2009).

The thinkers who could be loosely described as "new materialists" are far less concerned than the speculative realists are with the particular paradoxes of correlationism. But they also seek to elaborate new ways of grasping the world, outside of anthropocentric paradigms and grounded in a firm commitment to realism (for a survey of the various new materialisms, see Coole and Frost 2010 and Dolphijn and van der Tuin 2012). Most of the new materialists are strongly influenced (as Graham Harman is also) by the work of Bruno Latour. They take inspiration from the way that Latour traces the power struggles and negotiations of nonhuman as well as human actants (Latour 1988, 151–238) and envisions a world of proliferating hybrids (Latour 1993, 1–3 and passim). Thus Jane Bennett champions a "vital materialism" in which things exhibit "a positive, productive power of their own" (2010, 1 and passim). Rosi Braidotti similarly explores the possibility of a "vitalist materialism" that would involve "a nonhuman yet affirmative life force" (in Coole and Frost 2010, 203). Elizabeth Grosz, following up on suggestions from Bergson, proposes a notion of "freedom" that is "not tied to the emergence of reason, to the capacity for reflection, or to some inherent quality of the human" (in Coole and Frost 2010, 149). And Karen Barad proposes an "agential realism" in response to the continuing paradoxes of quantum mechanics (2007, 132–85).

In this book, I both reconsider Whitehead's thought in the light of speculative realism and new materialism and suggest revisions to these latter trends from a Whiteheadian standpoint. Let me summarize the remaining chapters briefly. The first chapter, "Self-Enjoyment and Concern," compares Whitehead's stance on aesthetics and ethics with that of the great French-Jewish philosopher Emmanuel Levinas. Of course, Levinas is not a speculative realist, but his concern with immanence and transcendence, his insistence on a presence in excess of any totality, and his vision of an encounter with the absolutely Other stand in the background of the contemporary critique of correlationism. The second chapter, "The Actual Volcano," draws an explicit contrast between Whitehead's process-oriented thought and the object-oriented ontology of Graham Harman. The third chapter, "The Universe of Things," works through Harman's reading of Heidegger, together with Whitehead's reading of British romanticism, in order to propose an aesthetic ontology that does justice both to objects and to processes, both to things and to experiences. The fourth chapter, "Panpsychism and/or Eliminativism," argues that once we have rejected correlationalism, or the correspondence of thought and being, then we are left with a stark choice between either outright eliminativism (implying that being is radically devoid of thought) or else a generalized panpsychism (proclaiming the immanence of thought everywhere). The fifth chapter, "Consequences of Panpsychism," offers an overview of recent philosophical discussions of panpsychism, or the thesis that mentality is a basic property of matter. Whitehead's own version of panpsychism is thereby presented as a form of antireductionalist naturalism. The sixth chapter, "Noncorrelational Thought," examines the problems in existing speculative realist accounts of thought. It proposes an alternative image of thought that is nonintentional, nonreflexive, and most often nonconscious: a kind of "autistic" thought that is not correlative to being but immanently intrinsic within it. The seventh and final chapter, "Aisthesis," uses this image of thought in order to propose an aesthetics that is not limited to human judgment and not centered on human subjectivity in particular.

The great poet Stephane Mallarmé once wrote that "*tout se résume dans l'Esthétique et l'Économie politique*" (everything comes down to Aesthetics and Political Economy). I take this aphorism as a basic ontological truth (though I make no effort to prove it in this volume). Ethics, politics, and epistemology are all determined "in the last instance" by economy: in human terms by the forces and relations of production and in cosmic terms by the "general economy" of quantum fields, energetic flows, and entropic processes. But alongside all this—coextensive with it, but irreducible to it—is the realm of inner experience, or of aesthetics. "Apart from the experiences of subjects," Whitehead writes, "there is nothing, nothing, nothing, bare nothingness" (*PR*, 167). In this book, I leave aside the truths of economics and energetics and focus on the equally important truths of Whiteheadian experience. In doing so, I arrive at a point where—as is also the case for Graham Harman, albeit for different reasons—"aesthetics becomes first philosophy" (Harman 2007b, 205).

1   SELF-ENJOYMENT AND CONCERN

IN "NATURE ALIVE," the eighth chapter of his last book, *Modes of Thought*, Alfred North Whitehead writes that "the notion of life implies a certain absoluteness of self-enjoyment . . . the occasion of experience is absolute in respect to its immediate self-enjoyment" (*MT*, 150–51). In other words, life is a process of pure auto-affection. It involves a "self-enjoyment" that is both "immediate" and "absolute." Self-enjoyment is "immediate" in that it happens prereflexively, in the moment itself. I enjoy my life as I am living it; my enjoyment of the very experience of living is precisely what it means to be alive: "The enjoyment belongs to the process and is not a characteristic of any static result" (*MT*, 152). Also, self-enjoyment is "absolute" in that it unfolds entirely in itself and for itself, without conditions. A living occasion is absolute in the etymological sense of this word: it is unbound, set free, released from all relation. Every moment of life is an autonomous "self-creation" (*MT*, 151). A living occasion must "be understood without reference to any other concurrent occasions" (*MT*, 151).

Just a few pages later, however, Whitehead says something quite different. He writes that "each occasion is an activity of concern, in the Quaker sense of that term . . . The occasion is concerned, in the way of feeling and aim, with things that in their own essence lie beyond it" (*MT*, 167). Now, for the Quakers, *concern* implies a weight on the spirit. When something concerns me, I cannot ignore it or walk away from it. It presses on my being and compels me to respond. Concern, therefore, is an involuntary experience of being affected by others. It opens me, in spite of myself, to the outside. It compromises my autonomy, leading me toward something beyond myself. Concern is relational, rather than absolute, and allo-affective, rather than auto-affective.

The distinction between self-enjoyment and concern is fundamental. Yet at the same time, these two conditions are closely bound together. You can't have one without the other. Concern is itself a kind of enjoyment, and it arises out of the very process of immediate self-enjoyment, for it is precisely when "engaged in its own immediate self-realization" that an occasion finds itself most vitally "concerned with the universe" that lies beyond it (*MT*, 167). Life in its self-enjoyment "passes into a future . . . There is no nature apart from transition, and there is no transition apart from temporal duration" (*MT*, 152). Even the most immediate self-enjoyment has the thickness of what Whitehead (following William James) calls the "specious present" (*MT*, 89), and in this "temporal thickness," it reaches out beyond itself (*PR*, 169). It may not have anything to do with "any other concurrent occasions," but it is deeply involved with the antecedent occasions from which it has inherited and with the succeeding occasions to which it makes itself available.

Thus self-enjoyment fills the specious present, but it is transformed into concern insofar as that present moment is carried away along the arrow of time. In the midst of my self-enjoyment, I am projected toward the future, and thereby I spend or expend myself. Conversely, concern or other-directedness is itself a necessary precondition for even the most intransitive self-enjoyment, for no present moment may be divorced from the pastness out of which, or against which, it emerges. The absolute self-affirmation of the living occasion arises out of "a complex process of appropriating into a unity of existence the many data presented as relevant by the physical processes of nature" (*MT*, 151). This process of appropriation is not always benign. Whitehead reminds us that "life is robbery" (*PR*, 105). Every "living society . . . requires food," and food can only be consumed through the "destruction" of other living societies (*PR*, 105). This is certainly the case not just for carnivores but for all heterotrophs. Nonetheless, without such processes of destructive appropriation, there would be no self-enjoyment and no "creative advance."

Concern and self-enjoyment are so closely connected because they are both movements, or pulsations, of *emotion*. On the most basic level, Whitehead says, "life is the enjoyment of emotion, derived from the past and aimed at the future. It is the enjoyment of emotion which was then, which is now, and which will be then" (*MT*, 167). The emotion felt by a living being always comes from somewhere else, and it is always going somewhere else: "It issues from, and it issues towards. It is received, it is enjoyed, and it is passed along, from moment to moment" (*MT*, 167). Emotion arises out of the very "process of appropriation" (*MT*, 151); it is enjoyed in the immediacy of the specious present, only to be passed along in the very next instant. Life is a passage through time, whose midpoint is the self-enjoyment of the immediate present and whose extremes are the concern that I feel for the past and the concern through which I give myself to the future. An occasion is self-constituted and self-reflexive in that it does not refer to, and is not concerned with, "any other concurrent occasions." But it *does* refer to, and it *is* concerned with, the occasions that precede it and that follow it. Such is the "vector character" of all experience (*MT*, 167).

The contrast between self-enjoyment and concern is not, in itself, anything new in Whitehead's metaphysics. The term *concern*, always qualified as being meant in the Quaker sense, does not appear in *Process and Reality*. But when it is first invoked in *Adventures of Ideas*, it is associated with concepts that are familiar from the earlier book. Whitehead uses *concern* to denote the "affective tone" that is an essential feature of any "subject–object relation" (*AI*, 176) or of any act of perception or prehension whatsoever (*AI*, 180): "No prehension, even of bare sensa, can be divested of its affective tone, that is to say, of its character as a 'concern' in the Quaker sense" (*AI*, 180). No occasion ever prehends another occasion neutrally and impassively; the emotion it feels for the other thing, in the very process of prehending it, *is* its concern.

For its part, the term *self-enjoyment* is only used sparingly in *Process and Reality*. But its few uses are significant. Whitehead writes of the "self-enjoyment of being one among many, and of being one arising out of the composition of many" (*PR*, 145); that is, the very process by which "the many become one, and are increased by one" (*PR*, 21) is already itself an instance of self-enjoyment. Later in *Process and Reality*, he writes of the way that "an actual entity considered in relation to the privacy of things . . . is a moment in the genesis of self-enjoyment" (*PR*, 289). Self-enjoyment in this sense is thereby caught up in "the antithesis between publicity and privacy," which "obtrudes itself at every stage" in Whitehead's cosmology (*PR*, 289): "There are elements only to be understood by reference to what is beyond the fact in question; and there are elements expressive of the immediate, private, personal, individuality of the fact in question" (*PR*, 289). The privacy of self-enjoyment and the publicity of what will come to be called *concern* are both dimensions of every single occasion. In *Modes of Thought*, therefore, Whitehead is not really saying anything new about the antithesis between self-enjoyment and concern—except that he expresses the distinction far more clearly and emphatically than in his earlier texts.

What changes, then, in Whitehead's later thought? I would like to suggest that the difference between *Process and Reality*, on the one hand, and *Modes of Thought*, on the other, is precisely a difference of emphasis: that is to say, it is a rhetorical difference. But this does not mean that the difference is insignificant or merely apparent. The very fact that language, for Whitehead, "is not the essence of thought" (*MT*, 35) and that "each phraseology leads to a crop of misunderstandings" (*AI*, 176) means that linguistic variations need to be handled with the utmost care. To my mind, the *specificity* of Whitehead's late writing lies not in any actual change of doctrine but precisely in a difference of phraseology, or tone, or literary style. *Adventures of Ideas*, *Modes of Thought*, and "Immortality" (*SP*, 85–104) express Whitehead's metaphysics with a different rhetoric and in a different *manner*. And that makes all the difference.

Gilles Deleuze credits Whitehead, like the Stoics and Leibniz before him, with inventing a *mannerism* in philosophy, a way of thinking "that is opposed to the essentialism first of Aristotle and then of Descartes" (Deleuze 1993, 53). A philosophy of processes and events explores manners of being rather than states of being, "modes of thought" rather than any supposed essence of thought, and contingent interactions rather than unchanging substances. It focuses, you might say, on adverbs instead of nouns. It is as concerned with the *way* that one says things as it is with the ostensible content of what is being said. Even if the facts or data have not themselves changed, the manner in which we entertain those facts or data may well change: "In fact, there is not a sentence, or a word, with a meaning which is independent of the circumstances under which it is uttered" (*SP*, 103). It all comes down to the *aim* of the living occasion in question, which Whitehead defines as the manner in which one particular "'way of enjoyment' is selected from the boundless wealth of alternatives" (*MT*, 152). A mannerist philosophy has to do with the multiplicity and mutability of our ways of enjoyment, as these are manifested even in the course of what an essentialist thinker would regard as the "same" situation.

Whitehead concludes *Process and Reality* with a grand vision of "God and the World," in the course of which he works through "a group of antitheses," expressing the "apparent self-contradictions" that characterize experience in its entirety (*PR*, 348). These antitheses consist of "opposed elements" that nonetheless "stand to each other in mutual requirement" (*PR*, 348). Such is the case with "God" and the "World" themselves, as ultimate terms in Whitehead's cosmology. But it is also the case, on a smaller scale, with self-enjoyment and concern, as I have been describing them. In such an antithesis, each of the terms would seem to exclude the other. Yet Whitehead requires us to think of them together, and further, he requires us to think of them without having recourse to the subterfuges of dialectical negation and sublation, on the one hand, and without abandoning them as unsurpassable aporias or blocks to thought, on the other.

How is it possible, then, to resolve such antinomies? (I use the word antinomies advisedly, in order to recall Kant's antinomies, which also have to be resolved without recourse to dialectical subterfuge.) The answer comes from Whitehead's understanding of process. "God" and the "World," the two ultimate terms of each antithesis, must be maintained in a "unity" together (*PR*, 348), even as they "move conversely to each other in respect to their process[es]" (*PR*, 349). This means that the relation between the conversely moving processes will alter in terms of strength, or degrees of difference, from one moment to the next. In any concrete situation, the opposed processes may either "inhibit or contrast" with one another to varying degrees (*PR*, 348). Whitehead therefore asks an evaluative question: are we faced with a situation of "diversities in opposition," producing inhibition, or of "diversities in contrast," forming an affectively compelling pattern (*PR*, 348)? The antithesis is resolved when the latter alternative is chosen or, better, when the former is transformed into the latter through a creative act. This is accomplished—not theoretically but practically—through "a shift of meaning which converts the opposition into a contrast" (*PR*, 348).

The injunction to convert oppositions into contrasts is a leitmotif of Isabelle Stengers's great reading of Whitehead (2011). I would like to extend Stengers's argument by suggesting that this injunction is the founding impulse behind Whitehead's later writings. *Adventures of Ideas, Modes of Thought*, and "Immortality" begin precisely at the point where *Process and Reality* ends: with the conversion of seemingly intractable conceptual oppositions into what *Adventures* describes as an aesthetic design of "patterned contrasts" (*AI*, 252). In *Adventures*—after recapitulating, with subtle modifications, the argument of *Process and Reality* (Part III, "Philosophical")—Whitehead begins an entirely new discussion of the complex relationship between Truth and Beauty (Part IV, "Civilization"). Aesthetic questions only hinted at in the earlier work now become a central speculative focus. Whitehead states that "Beauty is a wider, and more fundamental, notion than Truth" (*AI*, 265). He asserts that "Beauty is . . . the one aim which by its very nature is self-justifying" (*AI*, 266), so "any system of things which in any wide sense is beautiful is to that extent justified in its existence" (*AI*, 265). With regard to humanity in general, he proposes that "consciousness itself is the product of art" and that "the human body is an instrument for the production of art in the life of the human soul" (*AI*, 271). And most outrageously and hyperbolically of all, Whitehead insists that "the teleology of the Universe is directed to the production of Beauty" (*AI*, 265).

Such assertions pose a challenge to our twenty-first-century sensibilities. In our current condition of late (or post-) modernity, we tend to be deeply suspicious of the claims of aesthetics. We are still frightened by the specter of what Walter Benjamin, writing at the very same time that Whitehead was completing *Modes of Thought*, denounced as the fascist "aestheticizing of politics" (2003, 270). Today, even if we do not reject aesthetics altogether, we do not assign a teleology to it. We tend, at best, to subordinate aesthetics to ethics and to politics. And even within the aesthetic realm, we value the sublime over the beautiful. What are we to make, then, of the rampant and unapologetic aestheticism of Whitehead's later works? I think this question can only be answered by working through Whitehead's own specific accounts of the aesthetics of "patterned contrasts." The polarity between self-enjoyment and concern in *Modes of Thought* is, quite precisely, such a patterned contrast: that is, it is beautiful and it produces beauty. But what does it mean to read the economy of self-enjoyment and concern aesthetically rather than ethically?

I can best approach this question by comparing Whitehead with Emmanuel Levinas, whose thought has been so crucial for the "ethical turn" in recent humanistic studies. Levinas's major work, *Totality and Infinity*, precedes its discussion of ethics with an extended analysis of enjoyment, or what Levinas calls "living from" (1969, 110ff.). Levinas equates enjoyment with a primordial sensibility and with an openness to the world. He describes it as a process of *nourishment*: "the transmutation of the other into the same . . . an energy that is other . . . becomes, in enjoyment, my own energy, my strength, me" (111). Through this movement, "enjoyment is a withdrawal into oneself, an involution" (118).

Despite the vast differences in vocabulary and rhetoric, this analysis has much in common with Whitehead's description of self-enjoyment arising out of a process of appropriation. Both Whitehead and Levinas insist that our experience is in the first instance physical, corporeal, and embodied. They both say that while nourishment initially comes from elsewhere, its consumption is entirely immanent and self-directed: "The act nourishes itself with its own activity" (Levinas 1969, 111); "what was received as alien, has been recreated as private" (*PR*, 213). Whitehead and Levinas both emphasize the *satisfaction* that comes from the sheer fact of being alive: "Life loved is the very enjoyment of life, contentment . . . The primordial positivity of enjoyment, perfectly innocent, is opposed to nothing, and in this sense suffices to itself from the first" (Levinas 1969, 145). Whitehead and Levinas both find, in this experience of sufficiency and satisfaction, a precognitive, prereflexive, and aesthetic mode of subjectivity: an "I" of pure experience that does not take the form of the Cartesian *cogito*.

But everything changes when Levinas moves on to his great subject: the encounter with radical exteriority, with the Other, with the face. The appearance of the Other "introduces a dimension of transcendence, and leads us to a relation totally different from experience in the sensible sense of the term" (Levinas 1969, 193). The face of the Other, confronting me, "puts the I in question" (195), for it absolutely "resists possession, resists my grasp" (197). It is an otherness that I cannot take as innocent nourishment. I cannot transmute it into more of myself, more of the same, for "the face speaks to me and thereby invites me to a relation incommensurate with a power exercised, be it enjoyment or knowledge" (198). In this way, the encounter with the Other makes an ethical demand on me, one that marks me even if I refuse it. This encounter is a kind of primordial trauma: it suspends and overwhelms the innocence of "living from," the economy of sensibility, enjoyment, and satisfaction. The naïve self-presence of primordial sensibility is dissolved and replaced with a new sort of subjectivity: one that is always already in default, obligated to an "idea of infinity" that "exceeds my powers" (196).

The call of the Other in Levinas's philosophy is its own authority; once I have heard this call, I cannot escape it or ignore it. Even to reject it is still to acknowledge it in an inverted way; as Levinas shockingly says, "the Other is the sole being I can wish to kill" (Levinas 1969, 198). This is why, for Levinas, ethics precedes ontology and absolutely overrides aesthetics. I am always already responsible to, and guilty before, the Other—even when I deny or have no cognizance of being in such a state. There is no counterpart or equivalent in Whitehead's thought for such an overwhelming, unidirectional transcendence. For Levinas, something like "concern in the Quaker sense" is irreducible. I cannot shake it off; it unequivocally trumps self-enjoyment. The imperious demands of ethical transcendence interrupt, exceed, and cancel the simple pleasures of aesthetic immanence. The passage from enjoyment to concern and responsibility is an irreversible one, and for this reason, it cannot be described, or aestheticized, as a patterned contrast.

Is it possible to resist such a movement of transcendence? What is at stake here is not refutation and argument but a basic *orientation* of thought. Everything in Whitehead cries out against the unilateral thrust of Levinas's vision. Levinas conceives of a single, grand transition: something that does not happen in time so much as it determines and instantiates a new sort of time. The apotheosis of the Other ruptures linear, homogeneous clockwork time and installs instead an "infinite" or "messianic" time: a "discontinuous" time of "death and resurrection" (Levinas 1969, 284–85). For Levinas, in striking contrast to Bergson, "there is no continuity in being" (Levinas 1969, 284). Continuity is false because the appearance of the face ruptures it once and for all. This epiphany points to a radical anteriority: an instance that precedes and that can never be contained within the extended present time of lived duration.

Whitehead also rejects Bergsonian continuity, but he does so in a very different manner and for very different reasons. "There is a becoming of continuity," he writes, "but no continuity of becoming" (*PR*, 35); that is, continuity is never given in advance. "The ultimate metaphysical truth is atomism," but out of the basic atomic constituents of reality, "there is a creation of continuity" (*PR*, 35). Both continuity in space (which Whitehead calls the *extensive continuum*; *PR*, 61–82) and continuity in time (Bergsonian duration) must actively be *constructed* in the course of the "creative activity belonging to the essence of each occasion" (*MT*, 151). In other words, continuity is approximated through a series of discrete, punctual "becomings" and "transitions." Transition is the very basis of continuity; this means that the experience of transformation is not unique but common. Concern is not the result of some sublime epiphany; rather, it is an everyday experience. For Whitehead, even death and resurrection are commonplace occurrences. Objects endure by refreshing themselves continually. Everything is subject to a rule of "perpetual perishing," for "no thinker thinks twice; and, to put the matter more generally, no subject experiences twice" (*PR*, 29). If this is so, then there can be no single, specially privileged moment of transition and no radical alterity such as Levinas demands. Time is irreversible and irreparable, but there is no traumatic moment in which my sensibility would be breached and my primordial enjoyment definitively interrupted.

Whitehead therefore rejects any grand narrative of a passage from self-enjoyment to concern or from the aesthetic to the ethical. Just as every actual occasion has both a physical pole and a mental (or conceptual) pole, so too every actual occasion evinces both self-enjoyment and concern. Indeed, this is precisely why these terms form a patterned aesthetic contrast and not an irreducible ethical opposition. Whitehead refuses to choose between concern and self-enjoyment. Or better, he says that every actual choice—or *decision*, as he prefers to call it (*PR*, 42–43)—involves both. If Whitehead is on the side of aesthetics as opposed to ethics and on the side of immanence as opposed to transcendence, this is not because he would reject either ethics or transcendence. Rather, he finds an immanent place for transcendence and an aesthetic place for ethics. He insists that every occasion is already, by its very nature, a "conjunction of transcendence and immanence" (*MT*, 167). Indeed, "every actual entity, in virtue of its novelty, transcends its universe, God included" (*PR*, 94). But this transcendence is just the other side of an immanent, actual fact. An object is transcendent as a process of decision or "as a capacity for determination," but it is immanent as an already realized fact or "as a realized determinant" of other objects (*PR*, 239).

Similarly, Whitehead gives an aestheticized account of ethics. He never provides a Kantian, categorical basis for moral duty, nor does he ever mount a Nietzschean attack on conventional morality. Instead, he insists that fact and value cannot be cleanly separated. They are always intimately entwined, since value is intrinsic to existence: "everything has some value for itself, for others, and for the whole" (*MT*, 111). Revaluation is a basic feature of experience, since every actual occasion involves a new "valuation up" or "valuation down" of previously given elements (*PR*, 241). But this revaluation also implies a continuing obligation: "we have no right to deface the value experience which is the very essence of the universe" (*MT*, 111). Even amid a Nietzschean "revaluation of all values," there cannot be, and should not be, any "overcoming" of concern. In this sense, there is always something of an ethical relation to others or an ethical demand coming from others. Self-determination never occurs in a vacuum, and it is never entirely free from "robbery" or "destruction." Indeed, it is precisely because "life is robbery" that, for living organisms, "morals become acute. The robber requires justification" (*PR*, 105).

Concern is thus inherent to every actual occasion, and living things in particular require justification. Nonetheless, concern and justification cannot be preeminent in the way that Levinas demands, for concern still hinges on an "autonomous valuation" (*PR*, 248), which is the occasion's own ungrounded, aesthetic judgment regarding the *importance* of what it encounters. Whitehead insists on "the concept of actuality as something that matters, by reason of its own self-enjoyment, which includes enjoyment of others and transitions towards the future" (*MT*, 118). In this formulation, attention to others is itself a kind of enjoyment, and it is included within, rather than opposed to, an overall self-enjoyment. In this way, valuation is not the response to an inexorable demand made by the Other. It is rather a "sense of importance" (*MT*, 118), arising from an autonomous, self-generated *decision* about what matters. "The phrase 'intrinsic importance' means 'importance for itself'" (*MT*, 118); thus "each unit exists in its own right. It upholds value intensity for itself" first of all—although this also "involves sharing value intensity with the universe" (*MT*, 111).

For Levinas, responsibility produces value; for Whitehead, the process of valuation first generates any sense of responsibility. For Levinas, ethics suspends spontaneous action; when I am confronted with the face of the Other, all I can do is *respond* to its call. For Whitehead, to the contrary, ethics can only be the result of a spontaneous aesthetic *decision*. Ethics is not the ground or basis of value but rather its consequence. It is only out of the actual process of valuation, or of determining importance, that "the conception of morals arises" in the first place (*MT*, 111). It is only in consequence of its own decision that "the subject is responsible for being what it is," as well as "for the consequences of its existence" (*PR*, 222). And this process of aesthetic valuation and decision is performed without guarantees, and without subordination, by every actual occasion. Whitehead beautifully says that "the basis of democracy is the common fact of value experience" (*MT*, 111). Such a "common fact" itself comes first; it cannot be derived from, or subordinated to, an encounter with the Other.

From a Whiteheadian point of view, then, Levinas's subordination of immanence to transcendence and of self-enjoyment to concern is one-sided and reductive—just as a philosophy of pure immanence and positivity would also be one-sided and reductive. Levinas's claim for the priority of ethics is one more example of the "overstatement" that Whitehead sees as the "chief error" of so much Western philosophy: "the aim at generalization is sound, but the estimate of success is exaggerated" (*PR*, 7). Concern is important, but it cannot be separated from self-enjoyment, much less elevated above it. Whitehead insists that "at the base of our existence is the sense of 'worth' . . . the sense of existence for its own sake, of existence which is its own justification, of existence with its own character" (*MT*, 109). This means that valuation is singular, self-affirming, and aesthetic, first of all. Aesthetics cannot be superseded by ethics: "The essence of power is the drive towards aesthetic worth for its own sake. All power is a derivative from this fact of composition attaining worth for itself. There is no other fact" (*MT*, 119).

2 THE ACTUAL VOLCANO

ALFRED NORTH WHITEHEAD WRITES that "a new idea introduces a new alternative; and we are not less indebted to a thinker when we adopt the alternative which he discarded. Philosophy never reverts to its old position after the shock of a new philosopher" (*PR*, 11). In the last several years, such a "new alternative" and such a "shock" have been provided by the rise of speculative realism. The speculative realist thinkers have dared to renew the enterprise of what Whitehead called speculative philosophy: "the endeavour to frame a coherent, logical, necessary system of general ideas in terms of which every element of our experience can be interpreted" (*PR*, 3). In what follows, I will look closely at the version of speculative realism that has come to be called object-oriented ontology (OOO). Graham Harman was the initial exponent of OOO (Harman 2005; Harman 2011a); more recently, he has been joined by Levi Bryant (2011), Ian Bogost (2012), and Timothy Morton (2013). I will compare and contrast OOO with Whitehead's own "philosophy of organism." My aim is both to show how OOO helps us to understand Whitehead in a new way and, conversely, to develop a Whitehead-inspired critique of Harman and OOO.

Harman, like his fellow speculative realists, explores what it means to think about reality, without placing worries about the ability of human beings to *know* the world at the center of all discussion. He is a *realist* because he rejects the necessity of any "Copernican rift between things-in-themselves and phenomena," insisting instead that "we are always in contact with reality" in one way or another (Harman 2009b, 72). And his thought is *speculative* because it openly explores traditionally metaphysical questions rather than limiting itself to matters of logical form, on the one hand, and empirical inquiry, on the other. In this way, Harman (much like Bruno Latour before him) rejects both scientific positivism and "social constructionist" debunkings of science. Harman cuts the Gordian knot of epistemological reflexivity in order to develop a philosophy that "can range freely over the whole of the world" from "a standpoint equally capable of treating human and inhuman entities on an equal footing" (Harman 2005, 42). He proposes a noncorrelationist, non-human-centered metaphysics, one in which "humans have no privilege at all," so "we can speak in the same way of the relation between humans and what they see and that between hailstones and tar" (Harman 2009b, 124).

Harman gives Whitehead an important place in the genealogy of speculative realist thought, for Whitehead is one of the few twentieth-century thinkers who dares "to venture beyond the human sphere" (Harman 2005, 190) and to place all entities on the same footing. Whitehead rejects "the [Kantian] notion that the gap between human and world is more philosophically important than the gaps between any other sorts of entities" (Harman 2009b, 51). Or, to restate this in Whitehead's own terms, Western philosophy since Descartes gives far too large a place to "presentational immediacy," or the clear and distinct representation of sensations in the mind of a conscious, perceiving subject (*PR*, 61–70). In fact, such perception is far less common, and far less important, than what Whitehead calls "perception in the mode of causal efficacy," or the "vague" (nonrepresentational) way that entities affect and are affected by one another through a process of vector transmission (*PR*, 120ff.). Presentational immediacy does not merit the transcendental or constitutive role that Kant attributes to it, for this mode of perception is confined to "high-grade organisms" that are "relatively few" in the universe as a whole. On the other hand, causal efficacy is universal; it plays a larger role in our own experience than we tend to realize, and it can be attributed "even to organisms of the lowest grade" (*PR*, 172).

From the viewpoint of causal efficacy, all actual entities in the universe stand on the same ontological footing. No special ontological privileges can distinguish God from "the most trivial puff of existence in far-off empty space" in spite of all "gradations of importance, and diversities of function, yet in the principles which actuality exemplifies all are on the same level" (*PR*, 18). And what holds for God holds all the more for human subjectivity. Whitehead refuses to privilege human access and instead is willing to envision, as Harman puts it, "a world in which the things really do perceive each other" rather than just being perceived by us (2005, 52). Causal and perceptual interactions are no longer held hostage to human-centric categories. For Whitehead and Harman alike, there is therefore no hierarchy of being. No particular entity—not even the human subject—can claim metaphysical preeminence or serve as a favored mediator. All entities, of all sizes and scales, have the same degree of reality. They all interact with each other in the same ways, and they all exhibit the same sorts of properties. This is a crucial aspect of Whitehead's metaphysics, and it is one that Harman has allowed us to see more clearly than ever before.

It is in the context of this shared project that I want to discuss the crucial differences between Whitehead and Harman. Although both thinkers reject correlationism, they do so on entirely separate—and indeed incompatible—grounds. For Whitehead, human perception and cognition have no special or privileged status, because they simply take their place among the myriad ways in which all actual entities *prehend* other entities. Prehension includes both causal relations and perceptual ones and makes no fundamental distinction between them. Ontological equality comes from contact and mutual implication. All actual entities are ontologically equal because they all enter into the same sorts of relations. They all become what they are by prehending other entities. Whitehead's key term *prehension* can be defined as any process—causal, perceptual, or of another nature entirely—in which an entity grasps, registers the presence of, responds to, or is affected by another entity. All actual entities constitute themselves by integrating multiple prehensions;

they are all "drops of experience, complex and interdependent" (*PR*, 18). All sorts of entities, from God to the "most trivial puff of existence," figure equally among the "'really real' things whose interconnections and individual characters constitute the universe" (*MT*, 150). When relations extend everywhere, so that "there is no possibility of a detached, self-contained local existence," and "the environment enters into the nature of each thing" (*MT*, 138), then no single being—not the human subject, and not even God—can claim priority over any other.

For Harman, in contrast, all objects are ontologically equal because they are all equally *withdrawn* from one another. Harman posits a strange world of autonomous, subterranean objects, "receding from all relations, always having an existence that perception or sheer causation can never adequately measure . . . a universe packed full of elusive substances stuffed into mutually exclusive vacuums" (2005, 75–76). For Harman, there is a fundamental gap between objects as they exist in and for themselves and the external relations into which these objects enter: "The basic dualism in the world lies not between spirit and nature, or phenomenon and noumenon, but between things in their intimate reality and things as confronted by other things" (74). Every object retains a hidden reserve of being, one that is never exhausted by and never fully expressed in its contacts with other objects. These objects can rightly be called *substances*, Harman says, because "none of them can be identified with any (or even *all*) of their relations with other entities" (85). So defined, "substances are *everywhere*" (85). And in their deepest essence, substances are "withdrawn absolutely from all relation" (76).

The contrast between these positions should be clear. Whitehead opposes correlationism by proposing a much broader—indeed universally promiscuous—sense of relations among entities. But Harman opposes correlationism by depriviling relations in general. Instead, Harman remarkably revives the old and seemingly discredited metaphysical doctrine of substances: a doctrine that Whitehead, for his part, unequivocally rejects. Where Whitehead denounces "the notion of vacuous actuality, which haunts realistic philosophy" (*PR*, 28–29), Harman cheerfully embraces "the vacuous actuality of things" (2005, 82). White-head refuses any philosophy in which "the universe is shivered into a multitude of disconnected substantial things," so that "each substantial thing is . . . conceived as complete it itself, without any reference to any other substantial thing" (*AI*, 132–33). Such an approach, Whitehead says, "leaves out of account the interconnections of things" and thereby "renders an interconnected world of real individuals unintelligible" (*AI*, 132–33). The bottom line for Whitehead is that a "substantial thing cannot call unto [a] substantial thing" (*AI*, 133). The ontological void separating independent substances from one another cannot be bridged. An undetectable, unreachable inner essence might as well not exist: "a substantial thing can acquire a quality, a credit—but real landed estate, never" (*AI*, 133). The universe would be entirely sterile and static, and nothing would be able to affect anything else, if entities were to be reduced to a "vacuous material existence with passive endurance, with primary individual attributes, and with accidental adventures" (*PR*, 309).

Harman, for his part, makes just the opposite criticism. He explicitly disputes the idea, championed by Whitehead (among so many others), that "everything is related to everything else." In the first place, Harman says, Whitehead's "relational theory is too reminiscent of a house of mirrors." When things are understood just in terms of their relations, an entity is "nothing more than its perception of *other* entities. These entities, in turn, are made up of still other perceptions. The hot potato is passed on down the line, and we never reach any reality that would be able to anchor the various perceptions of it" (Harman 2005, 82). This infinite regress, Harman says, voids real things of their actuality. In the second place, Harman argues that "no relational theory such as Whitehead's is able to give a sufficient explanation of change," because if a given entity "holds nothing in reserve beyond its current relations to all entities in the universe, if it has no currently unexpressed properties, there is no reason to see how anything new can ever emerge" (2005, 82). Or as Bryant similarly puts it, "insofar as the relations constituting structure are themselves internal relations in which all elements are constituted by their relations, it follows that there can be no external point of purchase from which structure could be transformed" (2011, 209).

In this way, Harman and Bryant turn Whitehead's central value of *novelty* against him, claiming that Whitehead cannot really account for it. However, it should be noted that Whitehead himself is well aware of this objection. The "actual entities" that make up the universe, according to Whitehead, "perish, but do not change; they are what they are" (*PR*, 35). More generally, Whitehead adds, "the doctrine of internal relations makes it impossible to attribute 'change' to any actual entity" (*PR*, 59). Because "every actual entity is what it is, and is with its definite status in the universe, determined by its internal relations to other actual entities," we cannot look to these entities themselves for the source of change (*PR*, 59). If this were indeed all, then we would be eternally stuck with nothing more than what we have already. Whitehead's own account of change depends on the finitude of the actual entities: the fact that they do not subsist, but perish. The "universe of actual things" is always "evolving" (*PR*, 59) because determinate things must always give way to other, newer things.

In this standoff between Whitehead and Harman, or between the idea of relations and the idea of substances, we would seem to have arrived at a basic antinomy of speculative realist thought. Whitehead and Harman, in their opposing ways, both speak to our basic intuitions about the world. Harman addresses our sense of the *thingness* of things: their solidity, their uniqueness, and their *thereness*. He insists, rightly, that every object is *something*, in and of itself, and therefore an object is not reducible to its parts, or to its relations with other things, or to the sum of the ways in which other entities apprehend it. But Whitehead addresses an equally valid intuition: our sense that we are not alone in the world, that things *matter* to us and to one another, that life is filled with encounters and adventures. There is a deep sense in which I remain the same person, no matter what happens to me. But there is an equally deep sense in which I am changed irrevocably by my experiences, by "the historic route of living occasions" (*PR*, 119) through which I pass. And this double intuition goes for all the entities in the universe: it applies to "shale or cantaloupe" (Harman 2005, 83) and to "rocks and milkweed" (Harman 2005, 242) as much as it applies to sentient human subjects.

The same contrast can be stated in other terms. Isabelle Stengers has taught us, in the course of her reading of Whitehead (Stengers 2011), that the construction of metaphysical concepts always addresses certain particular, situated needs. The concepts that a philosopher produces depend on the problems to which he or she is responding. Every thinker is motivated by the difficulties that cry out to him or to her, demanding a response. A philosophy therefore defines itself by the nature of its accomplishments, by what it is able to disclose, produce, or achieve. For Harman, the urgent task for philosophy is to account for how two entities, isolated as they are from one another, can ever possibly enter into contact. How can objects—locked away in their lonely prisons, withdrawn behind their firewalls—ever reach out into the larger world at all? Harman develops a whole theory of "vicarious causation" (2007b), reviving the ancient doctrine of occasionalism, in order to give an answer to this question. That is to say, for Harman, the general situation of the world is one of objects isolated in their vacuums. Given this situation, any connection, or communication, between one object and another is an extraordinary, fragile, and contingent achievement.

But my own metaphysical problem is precisely the opposite of this. As I put it in my book *Connected* (Shaviro 2003), I feel that our fundamental condition is one of ubiquitous and inescapable connections. We are continually beset by relations, smothered and suffocated by them. We are always threatened by overdetermination. Today we are beset by the overcodings of ubiquitous flows of capital, as well as by the demands that all the entities we encounter impose on us and the claims that they make for our limited attention. No "firewall" is strong enough to shield my computer, or my ego, from all these relentless implications and involvements.

Far from seeing any metaphysical problem of occasionalism or vicarious causation, therefore, I can only wish that some of the causations that continually beset me were indeed vicarious and occasional—instead of being all too overbearingly efficacious. For me, then, the great metaphysical problem is how to get away from these ubiquitous relations, at least in part, in order to find a tiny bit of breathing room. It is only by escaping from these overdetermined relations, by finding a space that is open for decision, that I may ever hope to find either Adventure or Peace (to name the highest values that Whitehead cites in the concluding chapters of *Adventures of Ideas*; *AI*, 274–96). To my mind, relation and causal determination are our common conditions and maladies, and self-creation or independence is the rare, fragile, and extraordinary achievement that needs to be cultivated and cherished.

Where does this leave us? As Whitehead suggests, we should always reflect that a metaphysical doctrine, even one that we reject, "would never have held the belief of great men, unless it expressed some fundamental aspect of our experience" (*MT*, 100). I would like to see this double intuition, therefore, as a "contrast" that can be organized into a pattern rather than as an irreducible "incompatibility" (*PR*, 95). Whitehead insists that the highest task of philosophy is to resolve antinomies nonreductively, without explaining anything away (*PR*, 17). Such is the "shift of meaning," which "converts the opposition into a contrast" (*PR*, 348).

Harman himself opens the way, in part, for such a shift of meaning, insofar as he focuses on the atomistic, or discrete, side of Whitehead's ontology. Whitehead always insists that, in the basic makeup of the world, "the creatures are atomic" (*PR*, 35). And Harman takes the atomicity of Whitehead's entities as a guarantee of their concrete actuality: "Consider the case of ten thousand different entities, each with a different perspective on the same volcano. Whitehead is not one of those arch-nominalists who assert that there is no underlying volcano but only external family resemblances among the ten thousand different perceptions. No, for Whitehead there is definitely an actual entity volcano, a real force to be reckoned with and not just a number of similar sensations linked by an arbitrary name" (2005, 82).

For Harman, this is what sets Whitehead apart from the post-Kantian correlationists, for whom we cannot speak of the actuality of the volcano itself, but only of the problem of access to the volcano or of the way in which it is "constructed" by and through our apprehension and identification of it. But at the same time, Harman also sets Whitehead's atomism against the way in which, for the speculative realist philosopher Iain Hamilton Grant, objects as such do not exist absolutely or primordially but only "emerge as 'retardations' of a more primally unified force" (Harman 2009a). For Grant, as presumably for Schelling, Deleuze, and Simondon before him, there would be no actual volcano, but only its violent, upsurging action or its "force to be reckoned with."

The point is that even as Whitehead's actualism links him to Harman, so his insistence on processes and becoming—which is to say, on relations—links him to Deleuze and to Grant. Whitehead refers to the "'really real' things" that "constitute the universe" both as "actual entities" and as "actual occasions." They are alternatively things or happenings. These two modes of being are different, yet they can be identified with one another, in much the same way that "matter has been identified with energy" in modern physics (MT, 137). When Harman rejects Whitehead's claims about relations, he is not being sufficiently attentive to the dual-aspect nature of Whitehead's ontology.

This can also be expressed in another way. Harman skips over the dimension of *privacy* in Whitehead's account of objects. For Whitehead, "in the analysis of actuality the antithesis between publicity and privacy obtrudes itself at every stage. There are elements only to be understood by reference to what is beyond the fact in question; and there are elements expressive of the immediate, private, personal, individuality of the fact in question. The former elements express the publicity of the world; the latter elements express the privacy of the individual" (PR, 289).

Most importantly, Whitehead defines *concrescence*, or the culminating "satisfaction" of every actual entity, precisely as "a unity of aesthetic appreciation" that is "immediately felt as private" (PR, 212). In this way, Whitehead is indeed sensitive to the hidden inner life of things that so preoccupies Harman. Privacy can never be abolished; the singularity of aesthetic self-enjoyment can never be dragged out into the light.

But privacy is only one half of the story. The volcano has hidden depths, but it also explodes. It enters into the glare of publicity as it spends itself. If Whitehead recognizes that, in the privacy of their self-enjoyment, actual entities simply "are what they are" (*PR*, 35), he also has a sense of the cosmic irony of transition and transience. And this latter sense is something that I do not find in Harman. Whitehead insists that every entity must *perish*—and thereby give way to something new. Throughout *Process and Reality*, Whitehead keeps on reminding us that "time is a 'perpetual perishing,'" for "objectification involves elimination. The present fact has not the past fact with it in any full immediacy" (*PR*, 340). In this way, Whitehead entirely agrees with Harman that no entity can prehend another entity in its fullness. There is always something that doesn't get carried over, something that doesn't get translated or expressed. But the reason for this is not that the other entity somehow subsists, beyond relation, locked into its vacuum bubble. Rather, no entity can be recalled to full presence because, by the very fact of its "publicity" or "objectification," it does not subsist at all; indeed, it is already dead. The volcano explodes and other entities are left to pick up the pieces. This reduction to the status of a mere "datum" is what Whitehead calls, with his peculiar humor, "objective immortality."

All this follows from Whitehead's dual-aspect ontology: from the fact that his entities are also processes or events. But for Harman, actual entities only have one aspect: they are quite definitely, and exclusively, things or substances, no matter how brief or transient their existence (Harman 2005, 85). This means that Harman tends to underestimate the importance of change over the course of time, just as he underestimates the vividness and the extent of relations among entities. Although he criticizes Whitehead for reducing existence to an infinite regress of relations, Harman himself gives us instead an infinite regress of substances: "We never reach some final layer of tiny components that explains everything else, but [we] enter instead into an infinite regress of parts and wholes"

(85). Having declared all relations to be "vicarious" and inessential, he gets rid of the problem of explaining them by decreeing that *any relation must count as a substance*" in its own right (85; a stipulation that, Harman admits, could just as easily be inverted). But this move doesn't really resolve any of the paradoxes of relationality; it simply shifts them elsewhere, to the equally obscure realm of hidden substances. Harman accounts for change by appealing to the emergence of qualities that were previously submerged in the depths of objects, but he does not explain how those objects came to be or how their hidden properties got there in the first place.

This criticism can, again, be stated in another way. Harman fully approves of the "actualism" (Harman 2009b, 127–29) expressed in Whitehead's "ontological principle": the doctrine that "there is nothing which floats into the world from nowhere. Everything in the actual world is referable to some actual entity" (*PR*, 244). From this point of view, Harman rejects all philosophies of "the potential" or "the virtual": "The recourse to potentiality is a dodge that leaves actuality undetermined and finally uninteresting; it reduces what is currently actual to the transient costume of an emergent process across time, and makes the real work happen outside actuality itself . . . Concrete actors themselves are deemed insufficient for the labour of the world and are indentured to hidden overlords: whether they be potential, virtual, veiled, topological, fluxional, or any adjective that tries to escape from what is actually here right now" (2009b, 129).

All this is well and good, except that I fail to see why Harman's own doctrine of hidden properties should not be subject to the same critique. How can one make a claim for the actuality, here and now, of properties that are unmanifested, withdrawn from all relation, and irreducible to simple presence? Such properties are unquestionably *real*, but they are precisely not *actual*. But such a formulation—"real, without being actual"—is also how Whitehead defines the potentiality of the future (*PR*, 214) and how Deleuze defines the virtual (1994, 208). Once again, Harman has translated a problem about relations into a problem about substance.

And such a translation is, in itself, a brilliant creative act, since "there is no such thing as transport without transformation" (Harman 2009b, 76). But relocating a difficulty, and forcing us to see it differently, is not the same as actually resolving it.

Because he insists on enduring substances, as opposed to relations among "perpetually perishing" occasions, Harman underestimates Whitehead's account of change. For Whitehead, an entity's "perception of *other* entities" is not just the repetition and passing-along of preexisting "data." It also involves "an act of experience as a constructive functioning" (*PR*, 156). Indeed, Whitehead uses the term *prehension*, rather than *perception*, precisely because the latter conventionally implies merely passive reception. For Whitehead, experience is never just "the bare subjective entertainment of the datum" (*PR*, 157). It always also involves what he calls the "subjective aim" or "subjective form" as well: this is *how*, the *manner in which*, an entity grasps its data (*PR*, 23). And this manner makes all the difference. An occasion may be *caused* by what precedes it, but, as Stengers puts it, "no cause, even God as a cause, has the power to define *how* it will cause. Nothing has the power to determine how it will matter for others" (2009, 40; emphasis added). Prehension always involves a whole series of deliberate exclusions and inclusions, which lead to a *revaluation*: "By this term *aim* is meant the exclusion of the boundless wealth of alternative potentiality, and the inclusion of that definite factor of novelty which constitutes the selected way of entertaining those data in that process of unification . . . That way of enjoyment is selected from the boundless wealth of alternatives" (*MT*, 152).

For Whitehead no less than for Harman, then, every "transmission" and "re-enaction" (*PR*, 238) of previously existing data is also a process of transformative reinvention.

To prehend a datum is therefore already to "translate" it into a different form. Harman's worry is that, in a fully relational world, no such translation is possible. We are condemned to an endless repetition of the same. From Whitehead's point of view, however, this worry is misplaced. The problem is not how to get something new and different from an impoverished list of already-expressed properties; it is rather how to narrow down and create a focus from the "boundless wealth" of possibilities that already exist. Harman seems to assume a primordial scarcity, which can only be remedied by appealing to substances, with their hidden reservoirs of "currently unexpressed properties" (Harman 2005, 82). Whitehead, in contrast, assumes a primary abundance of "data": a plethora that needs to be bounded and made determinate. Where Harman sees "countless tiny vacuums" separating objects from one another (Harman 2005, 82), Whitehead sees the universe as a finely articulated plenum. There is no undifferentiated magma of being; even a volcano is a fully determinate entity. But there is also no gap to bridge between any one such entity and another, for "an actual entity *is* present in other actual entities. In fact if we allow for degrees of relevance, and for negligible relevance, we must say that every actual entity is present in every other actual entity" (*PR*, 50).

What keeps entities distinct from one another, despite their continual interpenetration, is precisely their disparate manners, or their singular modes of *decision* and *selection*. Novelty arises not from some preexisting reserve but from an act of positive decision. Even the sheer "givenness" of the world cannot be postulated apart from "a 'decision' whereby what is 'given' is separated off from what for that occasion is 'not given' . . . every explanatory fact refers to the decision and to the efficacy of an actual thing" (*PR*, 42–43, 46). But the act of decision is spontaneous; it cannot be predicted or determined in advance. All the materials of transformation are already at hand; there is no need to appeal to vast reserves of hidden qualities. What is needed is rather "some activity procuring limitation"; Whitehead emphasizes that he uses the word *decision* "in its root sense of a 'cutting off'" (*PR*, 43). A decision is thereby an act of *selection*, consisting in processes of choosing, adding, subtracting, relating, juxtaposing, tweaking, and recombining. This is the only way to account for novelty without appealing to anything that "floats into the world from nowhere." Something new is created each time that a decision is made to do things *this way* rather than *that way* or to put *this* together with *that* while leaving something else aside. Every such act is a new creation: something that has never happened before.

Whitehead thus envisions a dynamic world of entities that make decisions—or more precisely, of entities whose very being consists in the decisions they make. Harman's entities, in contrast, do not spontaneously act or decide; they simply *are*. For Harman, the qualities of an entity somehow already preexist; for Whitehead, these qualities are generated on the fly. Harman, as we have seen, discounts relations as inessential; his ontology is too static to make sense of them. In contrast, Whitehead's insistence on decision and selection allows him to answer William James's call for a philosophy that "does full justice to conjunctive relations" (1912/1996, 44) in all their "great blooming, buzzing confusion" (1890/1983, 462). Only such a philosophy can be "fair to both the unity and the disconnection" that we find among entities in the world (James 1912/1996, 47). Relations are too various and come in too many "different degrees of intimacy" (James 1912/1996, 44) to be reducible to Harman's caricature of them as reductive determinations.

For Whitehead, echoing James, "we find ourselves in a buzzing world, amid a democracy of fellow creatures" (*PR*, 50). Such a world is no longer human-centered: this is what unites Whitehead with Harman and the other speculative realists. In addition, such a world is one of discrete, individual entities, self-creating and self-subsisting to the extent that "every component which is determinable is internally determined" (*PR*, 47): this unites Whitehead with Harman's object-oriented approach, as opposed to other varieties of speculative realism. But the world envisioned by Whitehead is "perpetually perishing"; thereby it also promises a radically open future. And this is what divides Whitehead from Harman. Where Whitehead insists on both internal decision and external relation, Harman has room for neither. And where Whitehead is concerned with both transience and futurity (which he calls "creative advance"), Harman shows little interest in either of these. At his most Whiteheadian, Harman will concede that "when two objects enter into genuine relation," then "through their mere relation, they create something that has not existed before, and which is truly *one*" (2005, 85). But Harman seems to backtrack from this concession when he describes this new relation as yet another vacuum-sealed object and when he therefore concludes that objects can only interact in the "molten interiors" (189) of other objects. Harman strikingly asserts that "the interior of an object, its molten core, becomes the sole subject matter for philosophy" (254). But this is to affirm the actuality of the volcano only at the price of isolating it from the world and reducing its dynamism to a sort of sterile display—which is all that it can be, in the absence of its direct effects on other entities. For Whitehead, everything is already—outside and inside—a molten core, an actual volcano.

To sum up, it seems to me that all the problems that Harman discovers in Whitehead's thought, and in relationalist thought more generally, also plague Harman's own substance-based philosophy. If Whitehead fails to account for the actual nature of objects and for the ways that the world can change, then Harman also fails to account for these matters. But this can be put in positive terms rather than negative ones. Harman's difference from Whitehead, and his creative contribution to speculative philosophy, consists in the "translation" of the deep problems of essence and change from one realm (that of relations) to another (that of substances). These two realms, oddly enough, seem interchangeable—at least in an overall anticorrelationist framework. Given that "there is no such thing as transport without transformation," the only remaining question is *what sort of difference* Harman's transformation of ontology makes. I would suggest that the contrast between Harman and Whitehead is basically a difference of style, or of aesthetics. This means that my enjoyment of one of these thinkers' approaches over the other is finally a matter of *taste* and is not subject to conceptual adjudication. And this is appropriate, given that both thinkers privilege aesthetics over both ethics and epistemology. Whitehead notoriously argues that "Beauty is a wider, and more fundamental, notion than Truth" and even that "the teleology of the Universe is directed to the production of Beauty" (*AI*, 265). Harman, for his part, enigmatically suggests that, in a world of substances withdrawn from all relations, "aesthetics becomes first philosophy" (2007b, 205).

The difference between Whitehead and Harman is best understood, I think, as a difference between the aesthetics of the beautiful and the aesthetics of the sublime. Whitehead defines beauty as a matter of differences that are conciliated, adapted to one another, and "interwoven in patterned contrasts" (*AI*, 252) in order to make for "intense experience" (*AI*, 263). Harman, for his part, appeals to notions of the sublime: although he never uses this word, he refers instead to what he calls *allure* (2005, 141–44), or the attraction of something that has retreated into its own depths. An object is alluring when it not only displays particular qualities but also insinuates the existence of something deeper, something hidden and inaccessible, something that cannot actually be displayed. Allure is properly a sublime experience because it stretches the observer to the point where it reaches the limits of its power or where its apprehensions break down. To be allured is to be beckoned into a realm that cannot ever be reached.

It should be evident that beauty is appropriate to a world of relations, in which entities continually affect and touch and interpenetrate one another, and that sublimity is appropriate to a world of substances, in which entities call to one another over immense distances and can only interact vicariously. It should also be noted that the beautiful and the sublime, as I conceive of them here, are alternative aesthetic stances that work universally in relation to all entities and all encounters. They are not limited "to the special metaphysics of animal perception" but apply to "relations between all real objects, including mindless chunks of dirt" (Harman 2007b, 205). In addition, it is not the case that some objects are beautiful, while others are sublime. Harman includes comedy as well as tragedy, and cuteness and charm as well as magnificence, within his notion of allure (Harman 2005, 142). As for Whitehead, his notion of beauty includes "Discord" as well as "Harmony" and gives a crucial role to what he calls "aesthetic destruction" (*AI*, 256). Whitehead thus antici-pates Morse Peckham's argument that every innovation "entails an act of cultural vandalism" (1979, 275).

It would seem that we are left with a definitive antinomy between relations and an aesthetics of beauty on the one hand and substances and an aesthetics of sublimity on the other. I have already made my own decision on this matter clear: by the very fact of seeking to turn the opposition into a contrast, by admitting Harman's metaphysics along-side Whitehead's, I have thereby already stacked the decks in White-head's favor. I have opted for relations and not substances and for beauty and not sublimity. Evidently, any such gesture can and should be regarded with suspicion. As Kant says, we can quarrel about taste, but we cannot dispute about it. Speculative philosophy has an irreducibly aesthetic dimension; it requires new, bold inventions rather than paci-fying resolutions.

I would like to end this chapter, however, with one final aesthetic con-sideration. Twentieth-century aesthetics tended overwhelmingly to favor the sublime and to regard the beautiful as inconsequential and archaic at best and positively odious in its conciliatory conservatism at worst. Whitehead was working very much against the grain of his own time in his peculiar celebration of beauty. Harman's aesthetics of allure, on the other hand, fits very well into what is now an extended modernist tradition. I wonder, however, whether today, in the twenty-first century, we might be at the beginning of a major aesthetic revaluation. We live in a world where all manners of cultural expression are digitally transcoded and electron-ically disseminated, where genetic material is freely recombined, and where matter is becoming open to direct manipulation on the atomic and subatomic scales. Nothing is hidden; there are no more concealed depths. The universe of things is not just available to us but increasingly unavoidable. The volcano is actual, here and now; we cannot expect to escape its eruption. Our predominant aesthetic procedures involve sam-pling, synthesizing, remixing, and cutting and pasting. In such a world, the aesthetic problem we face is Whitehead's rather than Harman's; it is a question of beauty and patterned contrasts rather than one of sublimity and allure. How can recycling issue into creativity and familiarity be transformed into novelty? Through what process of selection and decision is it possible to make something new out of the massive accumulation of already-existing materials? Tomorrow, things may be different, but for today, at least, the future is Whiteheadian.

3 THE UNIVERSE OF THINGS

THE SCIENCE FICTION SHORT STORY "The Universe of Things," by British writer Gwyneth Jones (2011, 48–61), tells of an encounter between a human being and an alien. The story is part of Jones's "Aleutian" cycle: a series of novels and tales set in a near-future earth that is visited, colonized, and ultimately abandoned by an alien humanoid race. The Aleutians (as these aliens are called) have technologies that are superior to ours. Also, they are of indeterminate gender; human beings tend to be discomfited by this. If anything, the Aleutians seem to be vaguely more "feminine" than "masculine," but human beings usually refer to them with the pronoun "it." For both of these reasons, the Aleutians' presence on our planet is traumatic and humiliating. It's not that they do anything particularly nasty or unpleasant, but their very existence somehow diminishes us. We find ourselves in a position of abject dependency; even the most affluent white male Westerners must now count themselves among the ranks of the colonized.

The Aleutians' presence on Earth undermines our inveterate anthropocentrism. "Man" is no longer the measure of all things. We can no longer think of ourselves as being special, much less take ourselves as the pinnacle of creation. Modernity is often seen as a long series of displacements and decenterings of the human; just think of Copernicus, Darwin, and Freud, or, for that matter, Deep Blue defeating Garry Kasparov. All this culminates in the effortless superiority of Jones's Aleutians, which leaves us blank and at a loss. And this is not just a matter of first contact, which is so frequently mythologized in science fiction narratives. Jones's aliens stay on Earth for centuries. The fact of their existence never loses its disturbing edge, even as it comes to be woven into the habits and assumptions of everyday human life. In this way, the Aleutian cycle is a narrative about—among other things—the adjustments forced on us as we enter a posthuman era.

Within Jones's overall Aleutian cycle, "The Universe of Things" focuses on one of the most striking differences between the aliens and ourselves: the fact that their technology, unlike ours, is intrinsically alive. The Aleutians' tools are biological extrusions of themselves: "They had tools that crept, slithered, flew, but they had made these things . . . They built things with bacteria . . . Bacteria which were themselves traceable to the aliens' own intestinal flora, infecting everything" (Jones 2011, 52). In effect, the Aleutians literalize Marshall McLuhan's thesis that all media are prosthetic extensions of ourselves. The Aleutians exteriorize themselves in every aspect of their environment. Their networks extend far beyond their own bodies and immediate surroundings. They are even able to share feelings and memories, as these are chemically encoded in the slime that they exude and exchange with one another. In consequence, "the aliens could not experience being *a-part*. There were no parts in their continuum: no spaces, no dividing edges" (57). They are alive in the midst of an entirely "living world."

The living world of the Aleutians stands in sharp and bitter contrast to the way that we remain trapped by our sad Cartesian legacy. We tend to dread our own mechanistic technologies even as we use them more and more. We cannot escape the pervasive sense, endemic to Western culture, that we are alone in our aliveness: trapped in a world of dead, or merely passive, matter. Our own machines, Jones writes, "promised, but they could not perform. They remained *things*, and people remained lonely" (2011, 56). It seems to some of the people in Jones's stories that in contrast to this situation, "the aliens had the solution to human isolation: a talking world, a world with eyes; the companionship that God dreams of" (56–57).

"The Universe of Things" tells the story of a human auto mechanic whom an alien hires to fix its car. The mechanic, like most human beings, both regards the aliens with awe and at the same time feels a bit afraid of them. He is honored and humbled, but also made extremely anxious, when the alien entrusts the repair of its vehicle to him. He doesn't know why he has been singled out for this job, nor does he know why the alien uses an inferior (and ecologically harmful) Earth technology in the first place, instead of sticking with the Aleutians' own mode of living transport. In any case, the mechanic focuses all his confused feelings on the car. Wanting to maintain "the mystique of craftsmanship" (Jones 2011, 48), the one sort of human pride that remains to him, he turns off all the machines that usually do the repair work in his shop and resolves to fix the alien's car by hand.

In the course of a long evening, as he works on the car, the mechanic has an epiphany—or a hallucination. He experiences, for a moment, what the aliens' "living world" is actually like: his own tools seem to come alive. The experience is disconcerting, to say the least: "He stared at the spanner in his hand until the rod of metal lost its shine. Skin crept over it, the adjustable socket became a cup of muscle, pursed like an anus, wet lips drawn back by a twist on the tumescent rod" (Jones 2011, 58). The living world is obscene and pornographic. Existence is suffocating and unbearable. Everything is suffused by "living slime . . . full of self, of human substance, but somehow rendered *other*" (58). This is what happens when you have "succeeded in entering the alien mind, seen the world through alien eyes. How could you expect such an experience to be pleasant?" (58). The mechanic is terrified and nauseated. All he wants is to return to the loneliness and security of the customary human world: a world in which objects remain at a proper distance from us, because they are "dead, and safe" (58).

"The Universe of Things" encourages us to think about the liveliness of objects and about the ways that they are related to us. The story suggests that even when we have shaped things into tools and have thereby constrained them to serve our own purposes, they still have independent lives of their own. That is to say, tools (like things in general) are what Bruno Latour calls *actants*—just as much as we ourselves are (1988, 159). Things have their own powers, their own innate tendencies. When we make use of things, employing them as tools, we are really *allying* ourselves with them (Harman 2009b, 19). But alliance also means dependency; we discover that we cannot do anything without our tools' help. The story therefore posits something like what Jane Bennett calls *vital materialism*: the recognition that "vitality is shared by *all* things, and not limited to ourselves alone" (2010, 89).

But even as the story intimates this, it also dramatizes our fear of the liveliness of things. In the mechanic's experience, wonder turns into dread. The sense that everything is filled with "human substance" flips over into the paranoid vision of a menacing alien vitality. The magic of a fully animate world becomes a Cthulhu-esque nightmare. We are threatened by the vibrancy of matter. We need to escape the excessive proximity of things. We cannot bear the thought of objects having an autonomous life, even if this life is ultimately attributable to us. We are desperate to reassure ourselves that, in spite of everything, objects are, after all, passive and inert.

It is important that Jones's story is not about "things" in general; rather, it is specifically about *tools*, for tools are probably the objects in relation to which we most fully confront the paradoxes of nonhuman actants, of vital matter, and of object independence. Tools are extensions of ourselves, things that we have shaped explicitly in order to serve our own needs. They are supposed to be subordinate to our will. And indeed, most of the time, we don't even think about our tools; they are simply *there*. As Heidegger puts it—at least in the most common interpretation of his work— tools are ready-to-hand, available to us. Yet this very availability of our tools gives them a strange autonomy and vitality. We find that we cannot just *use* them. We must learn to work *with* them, rather than against them. We have to accommodate their nature and their needs, as well as our own.

My mention of Heidegger's *readiness-to-hand* (*Zuhandenheit*) is not just fortuitous; I think that "The Universe of Things" can well be read as an allegory of what Graham Harman, expanding Heidegger's concept, calls *tool-being* (Harman 2002). Harman explicitly criticizes the common reading of readiness-to-hand in pragmatic terms—which is the way I used the concept a moment ago. According to Harman, readiness-to-hand does not mean the practical handling of things, as opposed to their explicit theorization (2002, 125–26). Rather, the category of the ready-to-hand has a much broader reach. It does not consist "solely of *human devices* . . . We can speak of the readiness-to-hand even of dead moths and of tremors on a distant sun. As 'useless' as these things may be, they still exert their reality within the total system of entities" (152). Things are active and interactive far beyond any measure of their presence to us. Tool-being does not apply just to the human *use* of things; it is a far more fundamental ontological category. Jones's story begins with the familiar sense of tools as objects of use, but it culminates in the mechanic's discovery that the "universe of things" has a deeper reality.

The crucial point about tool-being, in Harman's analysis, is that it involves a radical *withdrawal* from simple presence and therefore from any possibility of theorization. Throughout Heidegger's work, Harman says, "the single error to be guarded against lies in the ingrained habit of regarding beings as present-at-hand, as representable in terms of delineable properties rather than acknowledged in the *actus* of being what they are" (2002, 27). Opposing this reduction, Heidegger always insists that "what exists outside of human contexts *does not have the mode of being of presence-at-hand*" (126). To reduce a thing to its presence-at-hand— which is to say to the sum of its delineable properties—is precisely to regard that thing as only the *correlate* of a consciousness perceiving it (Meillassoux 2008). But a thing is always more than its qualities; it always exists and acts independently of, and in excess of, the particular ways that we grasp and comprehend it. This is why Harman credits Heidegger with providing us with a way out from correlationism and toward an object-oriented ontology.

Harman argues that *all* entities are tool-beings; none of them may be simply reduced to presence-at-hand or to a simple list of properties. But tool-being itself is double: it has "*two* distinct senses. It is the performance of a withering subterranean force, but a force that also acts to summon up some explicitly encountered reality" (Harman 2002, 26). On the one hand, Harman says, "tool-beings . . . recede into the work of an unnoticed background . . . Dissolved into a general equipmental effect, entities vanish into a unique system of reference, losing their singularity" (44–45). This is what allows us to take our tools for granted; most of the time, we don't even notice them *as* objects. We rely on their equipmental effect, forgetting that this efficacy is itself the result of a vast network of alliances, mediations, and relays. Such is the initial, complacent assumption of the mechanic in "The Universe of Things."

But at the same time, and on the other hand, tool-being also involves a countermovement: a reversal. This is epitomized by Heidegger in the form of the "broken tool." When a tool, or a thing, fails to function as expected, then the excess of its being is suddenly revealed to us. As Harman wonderfully describes it, radicalizing Heidegger, there is "an uprising of distinct elements . . . a surge of minerals and battle flags and tropical cats into the field of life, where each object bears a certain demeanor and seduces us in a specific way, bombarding us with its energies like a miniature neutron star" (2002, 47). When this happens, the tool is *more-than-present*; it stands forth *too* actively and aggressively for me to posit it as present-at-hand. That is to say, the tool, or the thing, becomes *alive*—as the mechanic suddenly experiences in the story. And this uprising, or unveiling, is the very basis of object-oriented ontology, which Harman describes as an effort "to do justice to the distinctive force of these specific objects, to the eruption of personalities from the empire of being" (47).

I take this analysis, from the beginning of Harman's first book, *Tool-Being*, as fundamental—even though Harman himself rejects it. Although Harman starts out with Heidegger's understanding of the tool and the broken tool, he quickly moves onto different ground. The first part of *Tool-Being* describes a double movement: a retreat into the universal referentiality of equipment, or into "an oppressive totality withdrawn from view and devoid of particular beings" (Harman 2002, 47), followed by the eruption of absolute singularities, each object's emergence "defining a fateful tear in the contexture of meaning, the birth of an individual power to be reckoned with" (47). But in the course of the book, Harman collapses this dichotomy. He argues instead that the object's withdrawal from presence is a retreat from referentiality as well. This means that "the tool-being of a thing exists in vacuum-sealed isolation, exceeding any of the relations that might touch it" (287). Instead of swinging between an excess of referentiality on the one hand and an excess of singularity on the other, each object both disappears into and emerges out of its own inaccessible vacuum. Harman carefully notes that, as a result of this reformulation, "both Heidegger and Whitehead become direct opponents of my theory" (228).

I have taken Whitehead's side (and somewhat to my surprise, Heidegger's as well) against Harman in chapter 2; I will not pursue that line of argument here. Instead, I will simply continue to explore the further, positive implications of the double movement that Harman finds in Heidegger's account of tools and broken tools. Indeed, this doubleness is crucial to Jones's story. "The Universe of Things" turns precisely on the way that objects are irreducible to simple presence. It also suggests that this excess has two complementary aspects. The "universe of things" is, on the one hand, altogether systematic and auto-referential; as a ubiquitous medium, or extension of ourselves, it stretches well beyond whatever is immediately apparent or present. It turns on the irony that when "human substance" is everywhere, that substance gets stretched and scattered beyond recognition. This is the same process that McLuhan is getting at when he describes media as "the extensions of man" (1964/1994): media spread themselves out everywhere, and once we project them, they escape from our control and redound back on us, drawing us into new relations. "All media work us over completely," McLuhan says; "they leave no part of us untouched, unaffected, unaltered" (McLuhan and Fiore 1967).

On the other hand, the "universe of things" also shows itself in the obscene eruption of individual objects, in all their liveliness and singularity. When "all the tools . . . leap into action," the mechanic is assailed by "the ghostly feel of flesh in the machines" (Jones 2011, 58–59). In each of these machines, he finds a drop of self, a living will. His dread at this prospect exemplifies McLuhan's observation that the emergence of new media is "too violent and superstimulated a social experience for the central nervous system to endure" (1964/1994, 43). Such a heightening of contact with the universe of things is traumatic. The auto mechanic is reduced to nausea and panic. He has experienced the worst of both sides of tool-being. He is stifled by the "oppressive totality" into which his tools have withdrawn for their "equipmental effect." But equally, he feels menaced by the uprising of his tools as "distinct elements," flaunting their autonomy and demanding his attention.

The double movement of tool-being—as both retreat and eruption—points to two alternative but coexisting ways in which things are forever escaping our grasp. What retreat and eruption have in common is that they are alike irreducible to any correlation of subject and object, or of human perceiver and world perceived. They are both modes of escape from presence and from a human-centered context. If I cannot control and instrumentalize a thing, this is *both* because it draws me into extended referential networks whose full ramifications I cannot trace *and* because its singularity, bursting forth, stuns me in excess of anything that I can posit about it. Retreat and eruption are both movements by means of which things demonstrate that there is *more to them* than we can gather about them. A thing can never be fully defined by any list, no matter how extended, of its characteristics and qualities, for beyond all these, it has its own autonomous power. As Bennett puts it, "the capacity of these bodies [i]s not restricted to a passive 'intractability,' but also include[s] the ability to make things happen, to produce effects . . . All bodies become more than mere objects, as the thing-powers of resistance and protean agency are brought into sharper relief" (2010, 5 and 13).

Tool-being is therefore irreducible to use in the same way—and for the same reasons—that it is irreducible to presence. And this has a further, perhaps surprising, consequence. When objects encounter one another, the basic mode of their relation is neither theoretical nor practical and neither epistemological nor ethical. Rather, before either of these, every relation among objects is an *aesthetic* one. This is why, as Harman puts it, "aesthetics becomes first philosophy" (2007b, 205). Aesthetics is about the *singularity* and *supplementarity* of things: it has to do with things insofar as they cannot be cognized or subordinated to concepts and also insofar as they cannot be utilized, or normatively regulated, or defined according to rules. No matter how deeply I comprehend a thing, and no matter how pragmatically or instrumentally I make use of it, something of it still escapes my categorizations. Even when I obliterate a thing or consume it utterly, there is still something of it that I have not managed to incorporate, some force to it that I have not been able to subsume. Aesthetics involves feeling an object *for its own sake*, beyond those aspects of it that can be understood or used. The thing withdraws into its network, luring me into the shadows, and it bursts forth in a splendor that dazzles and blinds me. In both cases, the understanding is frustrated, and the will reaches the limits of its power. It is only aesthetically, beyond understanding and will, that I can appreciate the *actus* of the thing being what it is—what Harman calls "the sheer sincerity of existence" (2005, 135).

The dazzlement of things bursting forth is what Harman calls *allure*: the sense of an object's existence apart from, and over and above, its own qualities (2005, 142–44). Allure has to do with the showing-forth of that which is, strictly speaking, inaccessible; it "invites us toward another level of reality" (179). In the event of allure, I encounter the very *being* of a thing, beyond all definition or correlation. I am forced to acknowledge its integrity, entirely apart from me. Such an encounter alters the parameters of the world, tearing apart "the contexture of meaning" and rupturing every consensus. It introduces what Whitehead would call a *novelty*: a new entity, something that does not belong to the already-said and does not sit well within any previously agreed-on horizon. For Harman, allure is therefore "the engine of change within the world" (179).

But there is also a kind of aesthetic event that has to do with the retreat of things beyond our grasp, "into the work of an unnoticed background." This is what we might call *metamorphosis*, in contrast to allure.

Metamorphosis is a kind of wayward attraction, a movement of withdrawal and substitution, a continual play of becoming. In metamorphosis, it is not the thing itself that attracts me, over and above its qualities; it is rather the very unsteadiness of the thing that draws me onward, as it ripples and shifts in a kind of protean wavering. All the thing's attributes become unstable, as it slips and slides beneath them, retreating into the background, relating and referring beyond my capacity to follow. Metamorphosis thus reflects the way that, as Whitehead puts it, "every actual entity is present in every other actual entity" (*PR*, 50). In the movement of allure, the web of meaning is ruptured as the thing emerges violently from its context; but in the movement of metamorphosis, the web of meaning is multiplied and extended, echoed and distorted, and propagated to infinity as the thing loses itself in the network of its own ramifying traces. The auto mechanic in "The Universe of Things" is overwhelmed by both movements at once.

Both allure and metamorphosis are instances of what Whitehead calls "lures for feeling" (*PR*, 25, 184, and passim). This is one of Whitehead's most peculiar expressions, but I think that it well describes the basis of aesthetic attraction (and repulsion). A *lure* is anything that, in some way, works to capture my attention. It may entice me, or incite me, or seduce me, or tempt me, or compel me, or even bludgeon and bully me. But in any case, it addresses me from beyond. The lure is what Whitehead calls a *proposition*. Whitehead defines propositions (of which logical propositions are only a special case) as "tales that perhaps might be told about particular actualities" (*PR*, 256). In other words, a proposition proposes some sort of *potentiality* to me; it holds forth the prospect of a difference. And this potentiality or difference is always anchored in some "particular actuality," in an actual thing or a group of things.

Whitehead thus agrees with Husserl, Heidegger, and Harman that I do not encounter things just as bare packets of sensa or as present-at-hand bundles of qualities. Rather, we should say that things *proposition* me or that they offer me a certain "promise of happiness" (to cite Stendhal's famous description of beauty). The qualities of a thing—or more precisely, what Whitehead calls the "eternal objects" or potentialities that are incarnated in it—are only the bait that the thing holds out to me in order to draw me toward it. It may be that a particular thing dazzles me when it rises up from the depths, or it may be that it intrigues and bemuses me by withdrawing into endless labyrinths. But in either case, a lure has been "*proposed for feeling*, and when admitted into feeling it constitutes *what is felt*" (*PR*, 187). When I respond to a lure—and even if I respond to it negatively, by rejecting it—I am led to envision a possibility, or to "entertain a proposition" (*PR*, 188), and thereby to *feel* something that I would not have felt otherwise.

I think that the question of *feeling* is central here. Entities generally do not "know" one another; Harman is entirely right to say that a thing's reality is "irreducible to what is perceived of it" (2005, 187) and that when objects meet, they "fail to exhaust one another's reality" (188). But this cognitive and pragmatic failure is not the end of the story, for Whitehead suggests that entities interact by "feeling" one another, even in the absence of knowledge and manipulability. Things encounter one another aesthetically and not just cognitively or practically. I always feel more of a thing than I actually know of it, and I feel it otherwise than I know it. To the extent that I *do* know an object, I am able to put it to use, to enumerate its qualities, to break it down into its constituent parts, and to trace the causes that have determined it. But feeling an object involves something else as well. I feel a thing when it affects me or changes me, and what affects me is not just certain qualities of the thing but its total and irreducible existence.

In Whitehead's terms, our always-incomplete knowledge of things comes in the form of the "well-marked familiar sensa" of "presentational immediacy" (*PR*, 176). These are the ideas and impressions of the empiricists, the denumerable properties of an object. Presentational immediacy is the realm of Descartes's "clear and distinct" ideas; it is roughly equivalent to what Heidegger disparages as mere presence-at-hand. But things already affect one another prior to any such presentation of explicit qualities, in the mode of what Whitehead calls "causal efficacy." In this mode, "the inflow into ourselves of feelings from enveloping nature over-whelms us; in the dim consciousness of half-sleep, the presentations of sense fade away, and we are left with the vague feeling of influences from vague things around us" (*PR*, 176).

It is only in the realm of presentational immediacy, with its inevitable limitations and failures, that we are faced with Harman's paradoxes of "sensual objects" that must be distinguished from "real" ones (Harman 2007b, 176–81) and of occasionalism or vicarious causation (Harman 2005, 169–234). In the realm of causal efficacy, we have rather to do with a sort of total contact, a promiscuous interchange among objects. These encounters cannot entirely be cognized; they are never clear and distinct, but always leave us "prey to vague feelings of influence" (*PR*, 176). But the conceptual vagueness of these experiences does not lessen their power—quite the contrary. A feeling always involves some alteration of the one who feels. For Whitehead, experience is being; what an entity feels is what that entity *is*. This means that as the result of "entertaining" a lure, I have somehow been transformed—whether grandly or minutely. I have selected one definite outcome from among "the penumbral welter of alternatives" (*PR*, 187). As a result, I have become—however slightly or massively—a different entity from the one that I was before this happened. I am no longer the same as I might have been had I not been moved by this particular "flash of novelty" (*PR*, 184).

There is more than a hint of romanticism in Whitehead's notion of causal efficacy, just as there is in Heidegger's related notion of a world of equipment forming "a single gigantic system of references" (Harman 2007a, 62). The withdrawal of things into an ever-ramifying network of traces has much in common with the early nineteenth-century romantic idea of Nature—although today we should rather associate it with the mediasphere, or with the global financial network, or else with the World Wide Web, especially as it develops into what Bruce Sterling has felicitously called "the Internet of Things" (2005, 92–94). Whitehead makes this link to romanticism explicit when he points out how "the irresistible causal efficacy of nature presses itself upon us; in the vagueness of the low hum of insects in an August woodland, the inflow into ourselves of feelings from enveloping nature overwhelms us" (*PR*, 176). This vague sense of total envelopment is not peculiar to human beings; it extends throughout the natural world and is felt by animals and plants (*PR*, 176). Indeed, Whitehead claims that even inorganic entities experience something like an "influx of feeling," at least in the form of flows of energy, because "all fundamental physical qualities are *vector* and not *scalar*" (*PR*, 177).

In *Science and the Modern World*, Whitehead considers the romantic idea of nature at greater length. He does this in a chapter ("The Romantic Reaction," *SMW*, 75–94) that includes a discussion of several British romantic works. (This is one of the very rare cases in which Whitehead cites literary texts rather than philosophical ones.) One of the works that Whitehead examines is Percy Bysshe Shelley's poem "Mont Blanc"—the very text that provided Jones with the title for her short story. Shelley's poem begins with a description of how

> The everlasting universe of things
> Flows through the mind,

and it continues with an evocation of

> My own, my human mind, which passively
> Now renders and receives fast influencings,
> Holding an unremitting interchange
> With the clear universe of things around.

Whitehead remarks that, in spite of this poem's "explicit reference to some form of idealism," Shelley nonetheless "is here an emphatic witness to a prehensive unification as constituting the very being of nature" (*SMW*, 86). I think that this comment is worth unpacking. In place of *idealism*, we might today read *correlationism*, for the poem explicitly explores correspondences between the human mind as perceiving subject and the outside world as that which is perceived. Whitehead leaves open the question of whether Shelley's idealism is "Kantian or Berkeleyan or Platonic" (*SMW*, 86); subsequent scholarship suggests that Shelley rather advocated a kind of empiricism-turned-skeptical-idealism derived from William Drummond, a now largely forgotten disciple of Hume (Pulos 1954). In any case, the poem displays an overwhelming concern with subject–object dualism.

However, Whitehead suggests that the rhetoric of "Mont Blanc" undermines its apparent empiricism and idealism, for the poem states that it is actually "things" themselves—rather than their representations in the form of ideas or impressions—that flow through the mind. Shelley's insistence on a universe of actually existing *things* goes against the subjectivism and sensationalism of the rest of the poem, and of British empiricism more generally. (Whitehead defines *subjectivism* as the notion "that the datum in the act of experience can be adequately analysed purely in terms of universals" and *sensationalism* as the notion "that the primary activity in the act of experience is the bare subjective entertainment of the datum, devoid of any subjective form of reception"; *PR*, 157). To the extent that the poem envisions a "universe of things," it suggests that we perceive and respond to objects themselves: to the *actus* of their being what they are. We do not just analyze them in terms of universals by adding up and associating atomistic "ideas." My sense that "this stone is gray," for instance, is not a primary datum of experience but only "a derivative abstraction" (*PR*, 160). Implicitly for Shelley, as explicitly for Whitehead, all our mental impressions refer and belong to already-existing things: "the operations of the mind originate from ideas 'determined' to particular existents" (*PR*, 138). We do not just passively receive a series of bare, isolated sensa; rather, we actually do encounter Mont Blanc, with its surrounding glaciers and woods and waterfalls. The romantic experience of nature points us toward Whitehead's claim "that there are many actual existents, and that in some sense one actual existent repeats itself in another actual existent" (*PR*, 139).

"Mont Blanc" subverts its own explicit thematics in other ways as well. On one level, the poem is clearly sensationalist and correlationist; it posits a subject–object binary, with "my own, my human mind" passively registering impressions from "the clear universe of things around." But at the same time, the poem *also* suggests that not just "my human mind" but all entities without exception engage in the "unremitting interchange" of rendering and receiving "fast influencings." This is what leads Whitehead to say that nature, for Shelley, is "in its essence a nature of organisms" (*SMW*, 85), each of them separately perceiving, interacting with, and integrating its feelings of all the rest. More generally, Whitehead insists that "both Shelley and Wordsworth emphatically bear witness that nature cannot be divorced from its aesthetic values; and that these values arise from the cumulation, in some sense, of the brooding presence of the whole onto its various parts" (*SMW*, 86–88). These "aesthetic values" involve both allure and metamorphosis. Mont Blanc allures us as it "gleams on high," manifesting a Power that "dwells apart in its tranquility, / Remote, serene, and inaccessible." But this solitary, vacuum-sealed Power is also an actor in a vast web of interconnections: a force of metamorphosis that "rolls its perpetual stream" through all things, exceeding "the limits of the dead and living world," and even potentially working "to repeal / Large codes of fraud and woe." The separation of entities and their "cumulation" or interpenetration are two sides of the same coin; they are alike irreducible to subjectivism, sensationalism, and simple presence.

The interpenetration and "cumulation" of things in nature explains why, as Whitehead concedes, we often experience causal efficacy in the form of "vague terrors" (*PR*, 176). We are made uneasy when we feel "the haunting presences of nature" (*SMW*, 83) without quite knowing what they are. Things are just too suffocatingly close for us to be able to regard them as manipulable, or understandable, or present-at-hand. The intimacy of things is always discomfiting and uncanny; it can easily seem obscene and directly menacing, as it does to Jones's mechanic. McLuhan, in his account of oral, networked cultures, similarly suggests that "terror is the normal state" of a situation in which "everything affects everything all the time" (1962, 32). For Whitehead, things both differentiate themselves absolutely from one another and refer themselves incessantly to one another. The terror of interconnection is a kind of inverse, like a photographic negative, of the "satisfaction" with which an entity uniquely constitutes itself "into a completely determinate matter of fact" (*PR*, 212).

Whitehead thus insists on both the integrity of "particular existents" and "the brooding presence of the whole" of nature. This double assertion corresponds to the way that all entities perform a double movement of allure and metamorphosis, of bursting forth and slipping away, of displaying their absolute singularity and retreating into a maze of references and transformations. Each entity is "fully determinate" in and of itself (*PR*, 26), yet they all belong to a "*common world*" (*SMW*, 88–89). "The actual elements perceived by our senses are *in themselves* the elements of a common world," Whitehead says; "this world is a complex of things, including indeed our acts of cognition, but transcending them" (*SMW*, 88). We find ourselves always already "*within* a world of colours, sounds, and other sense-objects, related in space and time to enduring objects such as stones, trees, and human bodies. We seem to be ourselves elements of this world in the same sense as are the other things which we perceive" (*SMW*, 89). Things remain distinct from one another, but they are all "elements . . . in the same sense" of the same common world. This insistence is what links Whitehead to Deleuze, who also maintains that "being is said in a single and same sense" of all entities, even as these entities retain their difference from one another (1994, 42). The double movement of withdrawal and belonging is what makes possible a "democracy of objects"—as Levi Bryant beautifully calls it (2011). Or, as Whitehead puts it in *Process and Reality*, in a phrase that both refers back to and expands on William James, "we find ourselves in a buzzing world, amid a democracy of fellow creatures" (*PR*, 50).

I conclude this chapter with three points about this democracy of fellow creatures, this universe of things. The first point has to do with anthropomorphism, the second with vitalism, and the third with panpsychism. In the first place, throughout this discussion, I have freely used the first person; addressed issues of perception, knowledge, and feeling; and argued for the primacy of aesthetics. Does this not mean that I assume a human model after all, despite my rejection of anthropocentrism and correlationism? The answer is that, for Whitehead, as for object-oriented ontology, perception, feeling, and aesthetics are universal structures, not specifically human ones. This also means that aesthetics as a mode of contact between beings "belongs to ontology as a whole, not to the special metaphysics of animal perception" (Harman 2007b, 205). If all entities inhere in the world "in the same sense," then we must describe this inherence in the same way for all of them.

But if I am to conceive of other entities in the same way I conceive of human subjects, then my only alternatives are eliminativism and anthropomorphism. I can always follow the eliminativist, dismissing all accounts of human experience as misleading "folk psychology" and adopting the same reductive physicalist language to describe human behavior as scientists use to describe the phase changes of water. But if, together with Whitehead, I refuse to "indulge in brilliant feats of explaining away" (*PR*, 17), then I must accept that the categories I use to describe myself are also valid for other entities.

This means that every entity in the world has its own point of view, just as I do, and that each of them somehow *feels* the other entities with which it comes into contact, much as I do. As I have already noted, Whitehead "attributes 'feeling' throughout the actual world" (*PR*, 177)—though he doesn't claim that a stone's feelings are *conscious* in the way that a human being's are. The point is that a certain cautious anthropomorphism is necessary in order to avoid anthropocentrism. I attribute feelings to stones precisely in order to get away from the pernicious dualism that would insist that human beings alone (or at most, human beings together with some animals) have feelings, while everything else does not. As Jane Bennett puts it, "Maybe it is worth running the risks associated with anthropomorphism (superstition, the divinization of nature, romanticism) because it, oddly enough, works against anthropocentrism: a chord is struck between person and thing, and I am no longer above or outside a nonhuman environment. Too often the philosophical rejection of anthropomorphism is bound up with a hubristic demand that only humans and God can bear any traces of creative agency" (2010, 120).

In the second place, if all entities have feelings and exert agency, this means that they are all—at least to a certain extent—vital, active, and creative. This cuts against some of our most fundamental prejudices. Karen Barad observes that "the inanimate-animate distinction is perhaps one of the most persistent dualisms in Western philosophy and its critiques; even some of the most hard-hitting critiques of the nature-culture dichotomy leave the animate-inanimate distinction in place. It takes a radical rethinking of agency to appreciate how lively even 'dead matter' can be" (2007, 419). Getting rid of the living–nonliving distinction means that—as Bennett puts it—we can accept "neither vitalism nor mechanism" (2010, 62–81). Nineteenth-century vitalism, for instance, insisted on "a qualitative difference between entelechy-infused life and inorganic matter" (73). The former was supposed to be active and goal oriented, whereas the latter was regarded as passive and mechanistic. But twentieth- and twenty-first-century science makes this sort of distinction untenable. On the one hand, biochemistry since the discovery of the structure of DNA has shown that life activities are continuous with other physical and chemical processes; on the other hand, complexity theory and systems theory (not to mention quantum mechanics) have shown that even inorganic physical processes cannot be accurately conceived of in traditionally mechanistic and deterministic terms. Modern science discredits traditional vitalism, but it doesn't leave traditional mechanistic materialism in a much better position.

Contemporary philosophers of science have, of course, constructed reductionist theories that are no longer "mechanistic" in the old sense. However, if we are to accept the ontological dignity of things and not reduce them to being just the illusory effects of quantum fields, then I think we need to accept something like what Bennett calls *vital materialism*: the idea that "every thing is entelechial, life-ly, vitalistic" (2010, 89). Whitehead similarly suggests that "there is no absolute gap between 'living' and 'non-living' societies" (*PR*, 102); moreover, "we do not know of any living society devoid of its subservient apparatus of inorganic societies" (*PR*, 103). "Life" is therefore a matter of degree, of a *more* and a *less*;

it can only be identified relatively and situationally. There are many intermediate cases between life and nonlife: think of viruses, or of computer-based "artificial life." Even the simplest physical processes are more lively than we often realize, and even the most unambiguously living processes are always embedded within, and inextricably entangled with, comparatively nonliving ones. Vitality is unevenly distributed, but it is at work everywhere. This is why the "democracy of objects" is also a "democracy of fellow creatures."

In the third place, and most controversially, I think that vital materialism and object-oriented ontology both entail some sort of panexperientialism or panpsychism. This is obviously not a step to be taken lightly; it can easily get one branded as a crackpot. Most metaphysicians today, analytic or continental, science-oriented or not, tend to reject panpsychism out of hand. Indeed, in my own recent book on Whitehead, *Without Criteria: Kant, Whitehead, Deleuze, and Aesthetics*, I was quick to deny the panpsychist implications of his thought (Shaviro 2009, 28). I now think that my denial was wrong. For one thing, as David Skrbina (2005) has argued at great and persuasive length, panpsychism has a long history in, and is deeply embedded within, Western thought. For another, panpsychism has recently come to be entertained by thinkers of various persuasions, including analytic philosophers like Galen Strawson (2006) and, to some extent, David Chalmers (1997).

In the terms that I have set forth here, aesthetic experience is always asymmetrical; it needs to be posed in terms of a subject, as well as an object. A world of objects is really a world of experiencings; as Whitehead insists, "apart from the experience of subjects there is nothing, nothing, nothing, bare nothingness" (*PR*, 167). For Whitehead, "each actuality is essentially bipolar, physical and mental" (*PR*, 108); every actual entity has a "mental pole," at least incipiently. If we are to reject both the correlationist view that "the subject does not belong to the world: rather, it is a limit of the world" (Wittgenstein 1922/2001, sec. 5.632) and the eliminativist view that the subject is literally "no one" (Metzinger 2004), then we must discover an immanent sense of subjectivity, or at least of some mode of "having-experience." And if we accept Whitehead's ontological principle that "there is nothing that floats into the world from nowhere" (*PR*, 244) or Strawson's argument against radical emergence (2006, 12–21), then we must at least be open to the prospect that "having-experience" is already intrinsic to all existing actual entities. This proposition may serve, at the very least, as a lure for thought—a prospective consequence of the fact that we find ourselves in a universe of things.

4 PANPSYCHISM AND/OR ELIMINATIVISM

SPECULATIVE REALISM IS BEST ADDRESSED in the plural. There is not just one; rather, there are a number of speculative realisms. The four thinkers—Harman, Brassier, Grant, and Meillassoux—who spoke at the initial speculative realism conference at Goldsmiths College at the University of London in 2007 (Brassier, Grant, Harman, and Meillassoux 2007) in fact have vastly different positions and programs. And still more varieties of speculative realism have been enunciated since. What justifies uniting these diverse new modes of thought is that they have a common starting point. The four original speculative realists—Quentin Meillassoux, Ray Brassier, Graham Harman, and Iain Hamilton Grant—all reject what Meillassoux calls *correlationism*. In what follows, I will consider what positive positions this initial rejection commits us to.

Correlationism is not the same thing as the "bifurcation of nature" denounced by Whitehead (*CN*, 30). The critique of correlation and the critique of bifurcation arise from very different needs and concerns. Nonetheless, the two are not unrelated. It is only when our experience has been sundered in two that we could ever think of the need for a correlational structure in order to put it back together again. Modern Western thought, from Descartes through Locke and on to Hume, partitioned the world between primary and secondary qualities, or between objectively extended objects on the one hand and merely subjective "psychic additions" (*CN*, 29) on the other. This culminated in the crisis of Humean skepticism, which Kant resolved by arguing that the unknown realities "out there" must be organized in accordance with the conditions imposed by our minds. We have viewed the world through a correlationist lens ever since.

Correlationism might seem to be at odds with everyday common sense; most people, if you asked them, would unhesitatingly affirm that things outside us are real. Remember Samuel Johnson, who kicked a rock and claimed thereby to have refuted George Berkeley. Nonetheless, the idea that the world is necessarily beholden to our ways of shaping and processing it has indeed been the "default metaphysics," as Harman puts it, of the West for more than two centuries, ever since Kant (2009b, 25). To reject the correlationist consensus is to risk being accused of "naïve realism." In fact, no version of speculative realism actually maintains the "naïve" thesis that we can somehow have direct, unmediated access to a reality that is simply "out there" and apart from us. However, I also agree with Harman that we should be suspicious of any argument that disparages something by characterizing it as "naïve," for there is something disingenuous about such an accusation. Usually, the critics of "naïve realism" are not urging us to adopt a more robust or sophisticated sort of realism instead; rather, they are making the underhanded rhetorical suggestion that *all* realism is unavoidably naïve (Harman 2011c, 171). This critical sleight of hand really works to reinforce the solipsistic primacy of thought thinking only about itself. It is a way of refusing and denying any movement toward what Meillassoux calls "the great outdoors, the eternal in-itself, whose being is indifferent to whether or not it is thought" (2008, 63).

In any case, the basic speculative realist thesis is the diametrical opposite of the "naïve" assertion that things in themselves are directly accessible to us; the key point, rather, is that the world in itself—the world as it exists apart from us—cannot in any way be contained or constrained by the question of our *access* to it. "Man" is not the measure of all things. We habitually grasp the world in terms of our own preimposed concepts. We need to break this habit in order to get at the *strangeness* of things in the world—that is, at the ways that they exist without being "posited" by us and without being "given" to or "manifested" by us. Even the things that we have made ourselves possess their own bizarre and independent existence. If philosophy begins in wonder—and ends in wonder, too, as Whitehead insists (*MT*, 168)—then its aim should be not to deduce and impose cognitive norms, or concepts of understanding, but rather to make us more fully aware of how reality escapes and upsets these norms. This is why any true realism must be *speculative*—despite the fact that "speculation" has been held in ill repute for most of the past century. Confronted with the real, we are *compelled* to speculate—that is, to do precisely what Kant told us that we cannot and must not do. Pace Kant, we *must* think outside of our own thought, and we must positively conceive the existence of things outside our own conceptions of them. In Eugene Thacker's terms, it is not enough to just consider the (objective) world-in-itself in its difference from the (subjective) world-for-us. We must also actively explore what Thacker calls the *world-without-us*: the world insofar as it is subtracted from, and not amenable to, our own concerns (2011, 5–6). We learn about the world-for-us through introspection and the world-in-itself through scientific experimentation. But we can only encounter the world-without-us obliquely, through the paradoxical movement of speculation.

Speculative realism is therefore necessarily as far removed from post-Kantian "critical" thought as it is from "naïve" or unreflective thought. It rejects not only the "default metaphysics" of continental antirealism (Braver 2007) but also (and perhaps more important) what Jon Cogburn calls "neo-Kantian 'realism of the remainder' type realisms . . . the view that the real is some inarticulate and inarticulable mush" (2011). Slavoj Žižek, for instance, proposes that human subjectivity marks a unique rupture in the fabric of being. In the light of this continuing human exceptionalism, the Real can only be regarded negatively. It is nothing more or less than the traumatic remainder of a primordial split. The Real is what is left over from our separation from it. Since this Real resists all our symbolizations, Žižek says, it cannot be characterized at all (1993). For Žižek as much as for Kant, then, articulation and determination can only be found on the side of human access. Kant, after all, never denied that there was such a thing as a nonhuman Real. He maintained that things-in-themselves must really exist; he only insisted that we could not know anything positive about them or say anything meaningful with regard to them (as Meillassoux emphasizes; 2008, 31).

Let me rephrase all this as a formula. Philosophers have only *described* the correlationist circle, in various ways; the point, however, is to *step outside it*. The aim of speculative realism, as Meillassoux puts it, is to break free of the circle. Early modern philosophers like Spinoza and Leibniz exhibited a freedom, boldness, and daring that are scarcely imaginable today. More precisely, the question posed for speculation is how to attain this "precritical" freedom without reverting—as Meillassoux says we must not do—to any sort of precritical or pre-Kantian metaphysical "dogmatism." How, Meillassoux asks, can we "achieve what modern philosophy has been telling us for the past two centuries is impossibility itself: *to get out of ourselves*, to grasp the in-itself, to know what is whether we are or not" (2008, 27)?

In order to get beyond Kant's assertion of unknowability, or contemporary philosophy's disappointing "realism of the remainder," it is necessary to propose some sort of positive, speculative thesis alongside the negative (anticorrelationist) one. More precisely, every variant of speculative realism must maintain both a positive ontological thesis and a positive epistemological one. The ontological thesis is that the real not only exists without us and apart from our conceptualizations of it but is actually *organized* or *articulated* in some manner, in its own right, without any help from us. The epistemological thesis is that it is in some way possible for us to point to, and speak about, this organized world-without-us *without* thereby reducing it yet again to our own conceptual schemes.

What distinguishes the various speculative realisms from one another is that they each propose different ways of stepping outside the correlationist circle. The only thing that all these approaches *do* have in common is that they all return to the very starting point (the "primal scene") of correlationism: what Meillassoux calls the "Kantian catastrophe" (2008, 124). Kant's genius was his ability to negotiate successfully among the conflicting claims of the metaphysics of his time. He provided a settlement that reconciled the demands of both rationalism and empiricism while holding off the dangers of both dogmatism and skepticism. And correlationism was the price that Kant willingly paid in order to achieve this settlement.

Speculative realism therefore seeks to reopen the Kantian settlement and renegotiate it in a way that distributes its terms differently. And this redistribution opens up a place for renewed speculation. Meillassoux himself follows such a strategy. He disrupts correlationism from within by establishing that the Kantian correlation of thought and being is itself contingent (or "factial") rather than necessary. It happens to be the case for us, but it need not be. When we affirm *"the facticity of the correlation"* itself, we *"put back into the thing itself what we mistakenly took to be an incapacity of thought"* (Meillassoux 2008, 52–53). This is actually more of a Kantian maneuver than Meillassoux lets on. Whereas Kant, in his "Paralogisms of Pure Reason," demonstrates that certain fundamental metaphysical propositions are undecidable, Meillassoux traces this undecidability back to a more fundamental contingency. And this contingency turns out to be necessary in its own right: the one thing, according to Meillassoux, that *is* absolutely necessary. In his analysis of the paralogisms, Kant argues that the sort of logic that works in particular, limited empirical circumstances is no longer valid when applied to the world conceived of as a totality. Meillassoux follows a nearly identical line of argument when he shows that probabilistic reasoning, which is valid when applied to "objects that are *internal* to our universe," cannot be applied "to the universe *as such*" (Meillassoux 2008, 97). The difference, of course, is that Meillassoux draws on Georg Cantor's theory of transfinites (which was, obviously, unknown to Kant) in order to show that any sort of totalization is a priori impossible. This radicalization of Kant's own argument opens the way to a new kind of absolute knowledge: one that is free from Kant's strictures against it.

Iain Hamilton Grant similarly returns to the Kantian moment of decision, and orients it otherwise, when he reconstructs and revitalizes

F. W. J. Schelling's critique of Kant. The Kantian transcendental argument becomes a principle of genesis and productivity rather than one of a priori necessity. In consequence, thought does not—and cannot—posit or legislate the nature of appearance; rather, thought is itself generated through a process that is antecedent to it and that forever exceeds its grasp. It is a "necessary truth," Grant says, that "antecedence is non-recoverable" (in Bryant, Srnicek, and Harman 2010, 83). Somewhat like Meillassoux's ancestrality, Grant's antecedence cannot be recuperated in any sort of correlation. Yet the "unthought" of an infinitely productive Nature is not sheer negativity (as it remains for Hegel and for Žižek); rather, it is an active composition of powers or forces.

For his part, Harman proposes what I would like to call (echoing Derrida on Bataille) a "Kantianism without reserve." This consists in extending the gap between phenomena and noumena to the experiences of all entities. We can no longer specially privilege human beings (or rational beings in general), because every object encounters all other objects phenomenally only, as "sensual objects," without being able to reach those entities as they in themselves, noumenally, as "real objects." No object can ever entirely *know* (grasp or comprehend) any other object; indeed, an object cannot even really "know" itself. But Harman points out that we can, and do, *allude* to other objects: "relations between all real objects, including mindless chunks of dirt, occur only by means of some form of allusion" (2007b, 205). Indeed, we are alluding to objects— and objects are alluding to one another—almost all the time. We refer to objects that we do not know by designating them metaphorically or indirectly. In this way, we can be aesthetically *moved* by objects or causally *affected* by them even when we do not (and cannot) actually know or cognize them. Such *vicarious causation*—or what I would rather call *vicarious affection*—is a crucial mode of contact among entities. This is why "aesthetics becomes first philosophy" for Harman (2007b, 205), just as it does for Whitehead.

Brassier's physicalist revision of the Kantian distinction between phenomena and noumena can be contrasted with Harman's aestheticist one. Brassier converts Kant's "transcendental idealism" (as well as Deleuze's "transcendental empiricism") into a "transcendental realism" by asserting "the transcendental presupposition of an extra-conceptual difference between concept and object" (in Bryant et al. 2010, 56). That is to say, the real as such is nonconceptual, and the difference between the real and our concepts of it cannot itself be conceptualized. Our concepts are always inadequate to the objects that they refer to and that they futilely endeavor to circumscribe. Physical science is a way of exploring this gap between concept and reference—even if it can never bridge the distance altogether. Rather than thought imposing its categories on the real, Brassier says, in physical science "the reality of the object determines the meaning of its conception, and allows the discrepancy between that reality and the way in which it is conceptually circumscribed to be measured" (55). Kant's own defense of scientific objectivity is thus transformed into a more robustly realist form than Kant himself was able or willing to provide. Physical science is grounded in the inevitable failure of any correlation between thought and the world rather than in the necessity of such a correlation. The nonconceptual remainder is no longer mute, as it was for Kant and as it still is for Žižek; rather, scientific experimentation allows it (or forces it) to speak.

Other contemporary forms of realism also engage in revisions of this sort. The "critical realism" of Roy Bhaskar works by inverting the logic of Kant's transcendental argument. Bhaskar (1975) asks not what our minds must be like in order for the world to appear the way it does but rather what the world itself must be like in order for it to be able to appear to us in the way it does. Manuel Delanda offers a "reconstruction" of Deleuze's philosophy in the interest of uncovering a "realist ontology" that "grant[s] reality full autonomy from the human mind" (2002, 3). In order to accomplish this, he recapitulates Deleuze's own conversion of Kant from transcendental idealism to transcendental empiricism. Instead of transcendental conditions of thought that are imposed by the human mind, we have the realm of the virtual, which is objective and mind-independent and thoroughly real without being actual (Delanda 2002, 33, quoting Deleuze 1994, 208).

I have been insisting on the Kantian background of the speculative realist projects even though the speculative realist thinkers themselves often describe what they are doing in very different ways. I have done this because Kant's Copernican revolution in philosophy—or rather, his "Ptolemaic counter-revolution," as Meillassoux insists (2008, 117–18)—itself establishes correlationism and anthropocentrism on the basis of its own critical self-reflexivity. We should stop to think for a minute about how strange this is. According to Kant, thought does not discover its accordance with the world by reaching out toward the world; rather, it is precisely when thought reflects back on itself, when it engages in the critique of its own powers and limits, that it is suddenly brought into correlation with being. It is only by focusing back on itself, to the exclusion of all else, that thought comes into correspondence with something that lies outside it and beyond it. And it is this strange knot of thought and being—mirrored within thought itself by the preestablished harmony of inner-directed self-reflection with outer-directed intentionality—that speculative realism strives to undo.

In order to untie this knot of thought and being, it is necessary to dislodge the self-reflexivity of thought in one way or another. Thought needs to be radically problematized from the outside—instead of grounding and validating itself by means of its own purifying auto-critique. The anthropocentrism of our "default metaphysics," which Harman rightly finds objectionable, rests almost entirely on the dubious presupposition that human beings are uniquely rational, uniquely possessed of subjectivity and interiority, and uniquely capable of thought and/or language. Such a position was radically undermined by Darwin. And Whitehead entirely removes the need for it by elaborating an analysis of prehension that applies equally to all actual entities. Indeed, human exceptionalism is even less tenable today, now that we know that not only chimpanzees and parrots but also fruit flies, trees, slime molds and bacteria communicate, calculate, and make unforced decisions (Shaviro 2011).

But in fact, correlationism is not reducible to humanism or even to notions of subjectivity. As Meillassoux insists, "we must emphasize that the correlation of thought and being is not reducible to the correlation between subject and object" (2008, 7). Even the freeing of thought from subjectivity and from representation does not suffice to undo correlationism. Meillassoux gives the example of Heidegger, who rejects Cartesian and Kantian subjectivism but still insists on "the *co-propriation* (*Zusammengehörigkeit*) of man and being" (Meillassoux 2008, 8). Further, even the deconstruction and dissolution of the humanist subject do not really get us away from anthropocentrism: at best, they merely replace anthropocentrism with an impersonal noocentrism or logocentrism.

In order to step outside the correlationist circle, Meillassoux insists that we must displace thought (and language) altogether. We need to adopt a stance, he says, "which takes seriously the possibility that there is nothing living or willing in the inorganic realm" (Meillassoux 2008, 38). If we are to reject the phenomenological notion of "the givenness of the world," then we must recognize the existence of "a world capable of subsisting without being given to us or to any other perceiver: a world that is capable of existing whether we exist or not" (28). Reality for Meillassoux is "totally a-subjective" (38). We must "think a world that can dispense with thought, a world that is essentially *unaffected* by whether or not anyone thinks it" (116; emphasis added).

I believe that we need to take seriously this radical purgation of thought from being. Anticorrelationism can plausibly lead to radical eliminativism, as Meillassoux's formulations at least suggest and as Brassier argues much more forcefully and straightforwardly. For such an account, matter must be entirely impassive—devoid of life, initiative, or active force—in order to not be *affected* by thought. And sensation and perception need to be downgraded—or even abolished—because (like anything carnal) they imply an interaction between an observer and something being observed.

In his quest to guarantee the independence of being from thought, Meillassoux goes so far as to reintroduce into philosophy the explicit distinction between primary and secondary qualities (2008, 1–3). He privileges mathematical formalism at the expense of perception and sensation: this is the only way, he says, to "remove the observer," leaving behind just those properties that an object has in and of itself (1). *"All those aspects of the object that can be formulated in mathematical terms,"* Meillassoux writes—and *only* those aspects, we might add—*"can be meaningfully conceived as properties of the object in itself"* (3). Radicalizing Badiou's dictum that mathematics is ontology, Meillassoux argues that it is exclusively through "the mathematization of nature" that physical science indubitably allows us "to *know* what may be while we are not" (115). In effect, Meillassoux resolves the bifurcation of nature by brutally amputating the subjective side of the duality.

Brassier's arguments are similar to Meillassoux's but even more far-reaching. Once we accept that the difference of objects from the concepts we have of them is itself nonconceptual and not to be subsumed by thought, then we are forced to come to terms with "a world that is not designed to be intelligible and is not originarily infused with meaning" in any manner whatsoever (in Bryant et al. 2010, 47). This leads us inexorably to the "truth of extinction": the inevitable extermination of all thought in the future course of the universe (Brassier 2007, 205–39). Where Meillassoux points to that time before the emergence of thought that he calls the *ancestral* (2008, 10), Brassier points also to the distant future in which "the accelerating expansion of the universe will have disintegrated the fabric of matter itself, terminating the possibility of embodiment" (2007, 228).

For Brassier, even more than for Meillassoux, the recognition of a time altogether without thought must radically devalue thought in the present—and must even devalue this recognition itself. Unless we were to embrace some bizarre form of extreme idealism (thought without being?), we would seem to be condemned by the rejection of correlationism to a regime of being without thought. Undoing the Kantian nexus of thought and being leads us, in this case, to the conclusion that thought is epiphenomenal, illusory, and entirely without efficacy. Whereas Western science has traditionally seen mere matter as passive and inert, Brassier in effect argues that once we are rid of an unjustified anthropocentrism and narcissism, we must view human beings in this manner as well.

Brassier pushes this grim logic all the way to the end, proclaiming an "extinction of meaning that clears the way for the intelligibility of extinction. Senselessness and purposelessness are not merely privative; they represent a gain in intelligibility" (2007, 238). There is something impressively bracing about such militant nihilism, even if I am unwilling to give it the last word. But once we accept the anticorrelationist argument, what other alternatives can there be? Must the radical annihilation of meaning and purpose be the price we pay for understanding the real as it is, apart from us and from our correlations and projections?

In contrast to Brassier, Meillassoux evades the radical consequences of eliminativism by arguing for the absurd, radical emergence ex nihilo, at some point in the history of the universe, first of life and then of thought. As Harman makes evident in his recent exposition and partial translation of Meillassoux's otherwise unpublished manuscript *The Divine Inexistence* (Harman 2011b), Meillassoux insists—against all modern biology—both that life is radically discontinuous with mere matter and that thought is radically discontinuous with mere life. Meillassoux thus maintains the Cartesian picture of matter or extension as passive and inert, while providing an escape clause in the form of the absolutely contingent and unforeseeable coming-into-existence first of life and then of thought, both of which are irreducible to matter. This restores human exceptionalism with a vengeance. The violent audacity of Meillassoux's reversal reminds me, once again, of Kant. Just as Kant lets God back in through the back door, as it were, in the second critique, after having eliminated him in the first critique by destroying the ontological argument for his existence, so Meillassoux rehabilitates life and thought in *The Divine Inexistence* after having expelled them, together with the principle of sufficient reason, in *After Finitude*.

I am not willing, myself, to travel this route with Meillassoux. Despite his demonstrations of the contingency of the correlation and of the impossibility of transfinite totalization, I cannot see any justification for abandoning the principle of sufficient reason. Harman observes that Meillassoux has two objections to this principle. The first objection is that it implies an infinite regress of causes, unless we bring the regress to an end by arbitrarily positing a "first cause" or "unmoved mover." The second objection is that the principle implies that effects are *reducible* to their causes and that, if this were the case, then novelty would be impossible. But Harman replies that there is nothing wrong with conceiving an infinite regress and that an effect can well exceed its causes without thereby being entirely independent of those causes (2011b, 152–58).

Both of Harman's points are in accordance with Whitehead's revision and restatement of the principle of sufficient reason in the form of what he calls the *ontological principle*. According to this principle, everything that exists—every actual entity—has a *reason* (or more than one) for being what it is, and these reasons are themselves actual entities in their own turn: "Actual entities are the only *reasons*; so that to search for a *reason* is to search for one or more actual entities" (*PR*, 24). An actual entity may itself be one of the reasons for its own existence, alongside other (prior) actual entities. Everything is thereby *to some extent* self-caused (Whitehead refers specifically to Spinoza's definition of substance as *causa sui*; *PR*, 88). But there is no transcendent first cause independent of this process. For Whitehead, even God is a particular actual entity, the reasons for whose existence reside at least partly in other actual entities: "All actual entities share with God this characteristic of self-causation" (*PR*, 222). But also, conversely, God shares with all other actual entities the condition of being limited, and partly determined, by the actualities of "stubborn fact which cannot be evaded" (*PR*, 43).

In this way, Whitehead maintains a version of the principle of sufficient reason while at the same time insisting that nothing is ever *entirely* determined by its causes. An actual entity cannot evade the causes that feed into it, but it must decide *how* it receives and responds to these causes. More precisely, for a given subject prehending a given datum, there is always a certain degree of leeway in "*how* that subject prehends that datum" (*PR*, 23). And every such decision introduces at least a modicum of novelty into the universe. But the ontological principle also states that no entity can ever be entirely free from its antecedent reasons; "there is nothing which floats into the world from nowhere" (*PR*, 244).

Beyond all this, the real problem with Meillassoux's and Brassier's accounts is that they both assume that matter in itself—as it exists outside of the correlation—must simply be passive and inert, utterly devoid of meaning or value. But isn't this assumption itself a consequence of the bifurcation of nature? It is only an anthropocentric prejudice to assume that things cannot be lively and active and mindful on their own, without us. Why should we suppose that these are qualities that only we possess and that we merely project them on the "universe of things" outside us? Eliminativist arguments thus start out by presupposing human exceptionalism, even when their explicit aim is to humble and humiliate this exceptionalism. If you take it for granted that values and meanings are nothing but subjective human impositions, then it isn't hard to conclude that they are ultimately illusory for human beings as well as for other entities. The only plausible conclusion here is that of the early Wittgenstein: "The sense of the world must lie outside the world. In the world everything is as it is, and everything happens as it does happen: *in* it no value exists—and if it did exist, it would have no value" (1922/2001, sec. 6.41).

The radical alternative to this claim of valuelessness is Whitehead's vision of "the common fact of value experience, as constituting the essential nature of each pulsation of actuality . . . Existence, in its own nature, is the upholding of value intensity" (*MT*, 111). This means that value and sense are intrinsic to all entities and thereby immanent to the world as it actually exists. The world *as such* does not have any transcendent telos or values, because "the World" is not a singular entity: "The World is the multiplicity of finites, actualities seeking a perfected unity" (*PR*, 348–49). However, such a "perfected unity" is never achieved; "the World" never "reaches static completion" (*PR*, 349). Particular entities *within the world* do exhibit aims and values; this is what allows Whitehead to make such extreme, but also blandly generic, statements as that "creativity" is the "ultimate principle" of existence (*PR*, 21) and that "the teleology of the Universe is directed to the production of Beauty" (*AI*, 265), for even this latter "teleology" is characterless and generic rather than transcendent or totalizing. "Beauty," as Whitehead defines it, is nothing over and above "the internal conformation of the various items of experience with each other" (*AI*, 265). That is to say, "Beauty" for Whitehead is not an all-encompassing value but just a summation of the ways in which the multiple values of multiple entities strive both to maximize and intensify themselves and to accommodate themselves to one another. The crucial point is that since "existence" in its numerous instances involves "the upholding of value intensity," there can be no Humean separation of facts from values. And without the fact–value dichotomy, there is no need for the Kantian and Wittgensteinian resolution of the dichotomy by placing valuation "outside the world" or relegating it to the noumenal subject of practical reason.

What is needed to overcome the bifurcation of nature and to re-place value and sense within immanent experience is to find an alternative way of unbinding the Kantian knot of thought and being. And this is what Whitehead offers us, following William James. Rather than brutally purging the physical universe of anything like thought—an enterprise as absurd as it is ultimately impossible—James and Whitehead urge us to recognize the *commonness* and *ordinariness* of thought. They do not contest thought per se, as the eliminativists do, but only its self-reflexive self-privileging, its claim to specialness and preeminence. Isabelle Stengers observes that James engaged in "a deliberate project of the 'depsychologization' of experience in the usual sense of conscious, intentional experience, authorizing a clear distinction between the subject and its object." In this way, James "denied the privilege of occupying center stage to reflective consciousness and its pretensions to invariance" (Stengers 2011, 202; translation modified). Or, as James himself puts it, the reified entity known as *consciousness* "is fictitious, while thoughts in the concrete are fully real. But thoughts in the concrete are made of the same stuff as things are" (1912/1996, 37).

James's thesis is both monist (since everything is made of the same stuff) and pluralist (since there are many thoughts and many things, which cannot be gathered together as one). But it is antidualist and opposed both to the separation of fact from value and to the bifurcation of nature. Indeed, James positions his thesis in explicit opposition to what he calls the "neo-Kantian" doctrine that "not subject, not object, but object-plus-subject is the minimum that can actually be" (1912/1996, 5). In this way, James is an anticorrelationist avant la lettre.

James's characterization of *experience* provides the "prototype," as Stengers says, for Whitehead's "actual occasions" (Stengers 2011, 202). These are always "bipolar," with conjoined "physical" and "mental" poles (*PR*, 108). This means that thought is an immanent attribute—or a power—of being itself and of each individual entity that exists. Nothing could be further from the post-Kantian (or correlationist) sense of thought as something that would approach being from without and that would strive (successfully or not) to be adequate to it. For Whitehead, every entity immanently experiences something; or better, every entity *is* an experience.

This does not mean, however, that every entity is conscious. Whitehead insists that "consciousness presupposes experience, and not experience consciousness" (*PR*, 53). "In general," he says, "consciousness is negligible" (*PR*, 308), and even in beings like ourselves, it "only arises in a late derivative phase" of mental activity (*PR*, 162). Timothy Morton makes a more concrete, but somewhat similar, point when he suggests "that there is something that my mind does that isn't that different from what a pencil does when it rests on a table . . . It's not that pencils have minds, it's that minds are pencil like" (2011). Morton adds that he suspects "that consciousness is much 'lower down' than [cognitive researchers] deem to be the case." The point is that thought—whether or not it is "conscious" in the human sense—is common and humble rather than rare and preeminent.

Nonconscious experience is not an oxymoron; it is simply that more things are *felt* than can be known. Whitehead writes that "the primitive form of experience is emotional—blind emotion" (*PR*, 162). It is only in a few rare cases that this emotion is subsequently elaborated into self-conscious cognition. Emotional feeling, Whitehead says, is always "felt in its relevance to a world beyond," but "the feeling is blind and the relevance is vague" (*PR*, 163). Primordial "vector feeling," the physical movement or "transmission" from one thing to another, is undoubtedly the raw material out of which the whole drama of correlationism was constructed. But in its noncognitive, or precognitive, blindness and vagueness, thought as Whitehead describes it *happens*, or *passes*, without any epistemological warrant. It makes no sense for thought to be correlated to a world outside itself, for thought is already a constituent—we may think of it, perhaps, as a sort of flavoring—of the very world that it is supposed to be "about" and whose objects it is supposed to "intend."

We might think here of George Molnar's claim for the existence of what he calls *physical intentionality*. The commonly held doctrine, derived ultimately from Brentano, is that intentionality is an exclusive mark of the mental or psychological; indeed, intentionality is generally held to provide the definitive principle of a "*demarcation* between the psychic and the physical" (Molnar 2007, 61). Against this, however, Molnar argues that "something *very much like* intentionality" is a pervasive and ineliminable feature of the physical world (61). In making this point, Molnar strikingly anticipates Harman's argument against human exceptionalism. Even though "intentionality is regarded by almost everyone as a narrowly human feature," Harman says, in fact "intentionality is not a special human property at all, but an ontological feature of objects in general" (2007b, 189). This evidently blurs the line between mental properties and physical ones.

Molnar is a thoroughgoing realist about physical powers, or what analytic philosophers call "dispositions." He claims that "physical powers, such as solubility or electrical charge" (Molnar 2007, 63), actually exist as intrinsic properties of things. Most analytic philosophers today, like Hume two-and-a-half centuries ago, reject any such attribution. In their view, talk of powers has no meaning apart from the conditional statement that, for example, *if* the salt is put into water, *then* it will dissolve.

But Molnar rejects this sort of explaining away. He argues that powers, as intrinsic qualities of things, actually exist even at times when they are not being manifested or exercised.

It follows for Molnar that actually existing physical powers "also have that direction toward something outside themselves that is typical of psychological attributes" (Molnar 2007, 63). They have a sort of intentional structure: one that is not just outwardly directed but even "'determined' to particular existents" (to use a Whiteheadian phrase of which Molnar was probably unaware; *PR*, 138). Of course, physical intentionality, as Molnar describes it, is not likely to be conscious; it does not have any semantic or representational content. But Molnar points out that mental intentional states are not necessarily semantic or representational either. Pain, for instance, "is directed towards its intentional object"—the location where it is felt—"without representing (symbolizing) its object" (78). Although Molnar does not himself put it this way, the result of his argument is to *detranscendentalize* intentionality. That is to say, intentionality becomes an implicit striving-toward, or a potential for becoming, *within* the world, rather than being an underlying principle or structure of correlation. And in the process, intentionality also becomes a far weaker and vaguer concept than it was before.

Molnar admits that this extension and weakening of the notion of intentionality might lead to what he calls the "threat of panpsychism" (2007, 70). He pushes away this threat by replacing intentionality "with *another criterion of demarcation*" between mind and matter (71). The only other available criterion for mind, however, is precisely "the capacity for consciousness"—which Molnar embraces while acknowledging "that this position has its own distinctive difficulties" (71). If we accept that thought (or feeling, or experience) need not be conscious, then we might well be led to abandon the demarcation between mind and matter altogether.

Although Molnar himself is unwilling to embrace panpsychism, I propose that it gives us a good way to avoid the problematic baggage both of consciousness and of phenomenological intentionality. In this way, panpsychism might be a promise rather than a "threat." The non-eliminativist way of escaping the correlationist circle is to recognize the sheer ubiquity of thought in the cosmos. We don't need a criterion of demarcation because there is nothing to demarcate or separate. Once we understand "thought" in Whitehead's deflationary sense, rather than in Kant's grandiose one, we discover that it is everywhere rather than nowhere.

We can take an inverted clue here from Meillassoux. If we reject his thesis of the radical emergence of thought out of nothingness, then we must rather conclude that thought is always there already, in the very place where he claims that "there is nothing living or willing." This is basically Galen Strawson's position, as I will elaborate in the next chapter. Strawson argues that radical, "brute emergence" is impossible (2006, 12–24). Unless we accept Meillassoux's claim that things can and do happen for no reason whatsoever, then "experiential phenomena cannot be emergent from wholly non-experiential phenomena" (Strawson 2006, 24). Strawson regards eliminativism as absurd, "because experience is itself the fundamental given natural fact . . . there is nothing more certain than the existence of experience" (4). But because experience cannot float into the world from nowhere, our only alternative is to accept that reality is already experiential, all the way down.

Panpsychism, then, no less than eliminativism, undoes the Kantian knot of thought and being. A thought that is immanent to being is very different from a thought that must be correlated to being. In the former case, reflexivity drops out and intentionality is detranscendentalized, or even physicalized. Precisely because panpsychism claims that thought is always already present everywhere, it does not grant to thought any special foundational privileges. If mind is intrinsic to being, then it exists in and for itself, apart from any question of what it might be correlated with. In panpsychism, everything is mindful, or *has* a mind, but this does not necessarily entail that everything is "given" or "manifested" *to* a mind. I will discuss this in greater detail in chapter 7.

To conclude for now, I need to bring this discussion back to the initial speculative realist thinkers. Neither Harman nor Grant is a full-fledged panpsychist, but they are both inclined strongly in the panpsychist direction. This is evident from their essays in David Skrbina's anthology of contemporary panpsychist thought, *Mind That Abides* (2009). Grant indeed argues for "panpsychism all the way down, that is, without exception" (2009, 299), but in doing so, he complicates the question of emergence. Everything is in some sense minded or mindful, he says, but this mindedness is not there at the beginning; rather, it necessarily but belatedly arises from the antecedence of nature's productive powers. For his part, Harman sees mentality, or experience, as an inevitable component of any relationship or interaction among objects. But since he claims that objects are "withdrawn," existing apart from all relations, he doesn't attribute mentality or experience to these objects in and of themselves. There are undoubtably objects, he says, that remain "dormant," never entering into relation with anything else (Harman 2011a, 122–23); hence, for Harman, even "if all entities *contain* experience, not all entities *have* experience" (2009c, 282).

Despite these qualifications, I think that we are left with a clear alternative. If we are to reject correlationism and undo the Kantian knot of thought and being, no middle way is possible. We must say either (along with Harman and Grant) that all entities are in their own right at least to some degree sentient (active, intentional, vital, and possessed of powers) or else (along with Meillassoux and Brassier) that being is radically disjunct from thought, in which case things or objects must be entirely divested of their allegedly anthropomorphic qualities. When we step outside of the correlationist circle, we are faced with a choice between panpsychism on the one hand or eliminativism on the other.

This choice need not imply an exclusive either/or. Some of the more recent speculative realisms seem to combine the most extreme tendencies of both panpsychism and eliminativism—however oxymoronic such a conjunction might seem. I am thinking, for instance, of Ben Woodard's "dark vitalism" (2012), Reza Negarestani's "dark materialism" (2008), and

Eugene Thacker's "horror of philosophy" (2011). For these thinkers, the world-without-us is alien and actively hostile to human life and thought. If nothing else, such projects are further signs that we are beginning to think speculatively and cosmologically again—after a century in which, with the lonely exception of Whitehead, such efforts were viewed with suspicion and derision.

5 CONSEQUENCES OF PANPSYCHISM

WHAT IS IT LIKE to be a rock? Rudy Rucker's science fiction short story "Panpsychism Proved" (2007) provides one possible answer. An engineer at Apple named Shirley invents a new "mindlink" technology, which allows people to "directly experience each other's thoughts." When two individuals swallow "microgram quantities of entangled pairs of carbon atoms," they enter into direct telepathic contact. Shirley hopes to seduce her coworker Rick by melding their minds together. Unfortunately, he has other plans. She ingests a batch of entangled carbon particles, but Rick dumps his corresponding batch on a boulder. Instead of getting in touch with Rick, Shirley finds that "the mind she'd linked to was inhuman: dense, taciturn, crystalline, serene, beautiful." She fails in her quest for sex and deeper human contact, but she finds solace through intimacy with a "friendly gray lump of granite. How nice to know that a rock had a mind" (248).

Panpsychism is the thesis that even rocks have minds. More formally, David Skrbina (2005) defines *panpsychism* as "the view that all things have mind or a mind-like quality . . . mind is seen as fundamental to the nature of existence and being" (2). Or in the slightly different words of Thomas Nagel, who entertains the notion without fully endorsing it, panpsychism is "the view that the basic physical constituents of the universe have mental properties, whether or not they are parts of living organisms" (1991, 181). Most broadly, panpsychism makes the claim that mind, or sentience, is in some manner, as Rucker claims, "a universally distributed quality" (2006). In opposition to idealism, Cartesian dualism, and eliminativist physicalism alike, panpsychism maintains that thought is neither merely epiphenomenal nor something that exists in a separate realm from the material world. Rather, mind is a fundamental property of matter itself. This means that thinking happens everywhere; it extends all the way down (and also all the way up). There are differences of degree in the ways that entities think but no fundamental differences of kind.

Because it makes such seemingly extravagant claims, panpsychism is easily subject to derision and ridicule. The most common response to it is probably the one epitomized by the philosopher Colin McGinn, who calls it "a complete myth, a comforting piece of utter balderdash . . . isn't there something vaguely hippyish, i.e. stoned, about the doctrine?" (2006, 93). Even Galen Strawson, the best-known contemporary analytic philosopher to embrace panpsychism, admits that the doctrine "sounded crazy to me for a long time"; he finally got "used to it," he says, only when he became convinced that there was "no alternative" (2006, 25).

However stoned or crazy it might sound, panpsychism in fact has a long philosophical pedigree, as Skrbina amply demonstrates (2005). From the pre-Socratics, on through Spinoza and Leibniz, and down to William James and Alfred North Whitehead, panpsychism is a recurring underground motif in the history of Western thought. It was under eclipse in the second half of the twentieth century, but in recent years it seems to have returned with a vengeance. No less than three anthologies of essays on panpsychism have been published in the past decade (Freeman 2006; Skrbina 2009; Blamauer 2012), with contributions by analytic and continental philosophers alike. Panpsychism seems especially relevant today, in the light of the "nonhuman turn" in critical discourse and the growth of speculative realism. In any case, panpsychism has never been a mainstream philosophical doctrine, but it has persisted as a kind of countertendency to the anthropocentrism and hierarchical ontologies of dominant philosophical dogmas. Panpsychism offers a rebuke both to extravagant idealism on the one hand and to reductionism and eliminativism on the other.

The problem with panpsychism, for most people, is evidently one of *extension*. What can it mean to attribute mentality to all entities in the universe, without exception? Modern Western philosophy, from the Cartesian cogito through the Kantian transcendental subject and beyond, is grounded on an idealization of the human mind—or more narrowly, on the rationality that is supposed to be one of the powers of the human mind. And much of this tradition has sought to overcome the apparent problem of solipsism, or skepticism regarding "other minds," by appealing to a sensus communis, or a linguistic ability, that all human beings share. In this way, our minds are the guarantors of our commonality. But how far can the ascription of mentality be extended beyond the human? To begin with, can I rightly say that my cat thinks and feels?

Many philosophers have in fact said no. Descartes notoriously argued that animals were nonthinking automata. Heidegger maintained that animals (in contrast to human beings) were intrinsically "poor in world." Recent thinkers as diverse as Richard Rorty, Jacques Rancière, and Slavoj Žižek continue to endorse human exceptionalism because they all insist on the centrality of linguistic forms (conversation for Rorty, linguistic competence for Rancière, or the symbolic order for Žižek) as the basis for a sort of Kantian universal communicability. Even today, it is still often argued that nonhuman animals do not *really* think, because they are incapable of language, or because they do not have an awareness of mortality, or because they supposedly lack the capacity to make rational inferences. Robert Brandom, for instance, distinguishes mere *sentience*—or "mammalian sensuousness," such as my cat might feel—from the *sapience* that supposedly human beings alone possess; for Brandom, only the latter is *morally* significant (Brandom 2009, 148; see also Cogburn 2010 and Wolfendale 2010). Following Brandom, Pete Wolfendale argues that "nothing has value for animals, because there's no sense in which their behaviour could be justified or unjustified. This is the essence of the difference between us and them: animals merely *behave*, whereas we *act*" (2012).

In spite of such arguments, both philosophical claims and common opinion have shifted in recent years more fully in favor of recognizing the mentality of at least the higher animals (mammals and birds and possibly cephalopods). I presume that most people today would agree that dogs and cats have minds. That is to say, these animals think and feel; they have inner qualitative experiences, they register pleasure and pain, and they make decisions. But does a lobster similarly think and feel? Does a jellyfish? Does a tree? Does the slime mold *Physarum polycephalum*? In fact, there is good scientific evidence that *all* living organisms—including such brainless ones as plants, slime molds, and bacteria—exhibit at least a certain degree of sentience, cognition, decision making, and will (Trewavas and Baluška 2011; see also Shaviro 2011). But what about things that are not alive? How many nonstoned people will agree with Rucker that a rock has a mind? Or, for that matter, that a neutrino has a mind? According to Whitehead, Leibniz "explained what it must be like to be an atom. Lucretius tells us what an atom looks like to others, and Leibniz tells us how an atom is feeling about itself" (*AI*, 132). But who today is Leibnizian and Whiteheadian enough to assert that an atom, or a neutrino, feels anything whatsoever about itself?

Few advocates of panpsychism would expect that the doctrine could literally be verified by a scientific experiment, as happens in Rucker's whimsical story, for panpsychism makes an ontological claim rather than a necessarily empirical one. Even if we were able, as Whitehead once put it, to "ask a stone to record its autobiography" (*PR*, 15), the results would probably not be very edifying or exciting. It is not a question, therefore, of actually getting a rock or a neutrino to speak but rather one of recognizing that mentality, or inner experience, is not contingent on the ability to speak in the first place. Indeed, direct telepathic contact—like that portrayed in Rucker's story—is not likely to be possible, even between speaking human subjects. This is because any such contact would end up being public and external, precisely in the way that speech already is. Inner experience—sensations, qualia, and the like—would remain untouched. Panpsychism is not predicated on the possibility of what Graham Harman calls "human access" (2009b, 152–53 and passim) to other entities and other minds, whether human or nonhuman. To the contrary, panpsychism's insistence on the mentality of other entities in the world also implies the autonomy of all those entities from our apprehension—and perhaps even from our concern.

When panpsychism insists on the mentality of lobsters, neutrinos, and lumps of granite, what it is saying in the first instance is that these entities exist *pour soi* as well as *en soi*. They are autonomous centers of *value*. By this, I mean that it is a matter not just of how *we* value lobsters, or neutrinos, or lumps of granite but also of the ways in which these entities *value themselves*—and differentially value whatever other entities they may happen to encounter. For entities do indeed value themselves. In the first instance, they do so by the very act of persisting through time and establishing themselves as what Whitehead calls "enduring objects" (*PR*, 35, 109). This active persistence is more or less what Spinoza calls *conatus*, or what Levi Bryant calls the "ongoing autopoiesis" of objects (Bryant 2011, 143). I am not entirely happy with these terms, however. *Conatus* and *autopoiesis* seem to me to put too exclusive an emphasis on the entity's self-reproduction and maintenance of its identity, or on what Bryant calls its "endo-consistency" (141). But the value activity of an entity that persists through time is not just a matter of self-perpetuation or of the continually renewed achievement of homeostatic equilibrium. It may well also involve growth or shrinkage and assimilation or expulsion, or an active self-transformation and becoming-other. All these can be characterized as what Whitehead calls "conceptual initiative," or "the origination of conceptual novelty" (*PR*, 102). Such processes are more akin to what Gilbert Simondon calls *individuation* (2005), and to what the Whitehead-ian poet Charles Olson calls "the will to change" (1987, 86), than they are to conatus or autopoiesis.

In any case, the active self-valuation of all entities is in fact the best warrant for their sentience, for "value activity" is a matter of feeling and sometimes responding. Whitehead defines value, or worth, as an entity's "sense of existence for its own sake, of existence which is its own justification, of existence with its own character" (*MT*, 109). Each cat or dog has "its own character," and so does each lobster and each bacterium.

For Whitehead, "the common fact of value experience" constitutes "the essential nature of each pulsation of actuality. Everything has some value for itself, for others, and for the whole . . . Existence, in its own nature, is the upholding of value intensity . . . [Every entity] upholds value intensity for itself" (*MT*, 111).

In other words, each entity has its own particular needs and desires, which issue forth in its own affirmations of value. These are bound up in the very being of the entities themselves. Rather than saying (with Hume) that values cannot be derived from facts, or (with the early Wittgenstein) that value "must lie outside the world" (Wittgenstein 1922/2001, sec. 6.41), we should rather say that multiple values and acts of valuation are themselves irrefutable facts within the world. These values and valuations all *belong* to "a common world," as Whitehead says (*SMW*, 90)—indeed, they are immanent to the very world we live in. But each of these values and valuations also exists in its own right, entirely apart from us, and the values of other entities would still continue to exist in the world without us. The problem, then, is not to derive an "ought" from an "is" but to see how innumerable "oughts" already *are*. Contra Wolfendale, nonhuman animals *do* continually ascribe value to things and make decisions about them—even if they do not offer the sorts of discursive justifications for their value-laden actions that human beings occasionally do. And contra Brandom, this is indeed a morally significant fact, for as Whitehead puts it, "we have no right to deface the value experience which is the very essence of the universe" (*MT*, 111).

The standard retort to the Whiteheadian value argument that I have just been making is, of course, to accuse it of anthropomorphism. When Whitehead claims that nonhuman entities have values and experiences, that they have particular points of view, and that they think and make decisions, is he not imputing human categories to them? I would argue, however, that making such a charge is begging the question, for the accusation of anthropomorphism rests on the prior assumption that thought, value, and experience are essentially, or exclusively, human to begin with, and I can see no justification for this. Our own value activities arose out of, and still remain in continuity with, nonhuman ones—as we have known at least since Darwin. We perpetuate anthropocentrism in an inverted form when we take it for granted that a world without us, a world from which *our own* values have been subtracted, is therefore a world devoid of values altogether. After all, even Cthulhu has its own values—however much we may dislike them and (rightly) feel threatened by them. The same goes for the anopheles mosquito and for the (recently exterminated) smallpox virus. I think that this persistence of nonhuman values is a serious problem for the "eliminativist" versions of speculative realism, such as those of Quentin Meillassoux (2008) and Ray Brassier (2007). There is no reason why overcoming what Meillassoux calls "the correlation between thinking and being" (2008, 5) should require the extirpation of thought (or knowledge, or experience) altogether.

For a more nuanced approach to the question of nonhuman minds and nonhuman values, I turn to Thomas Nagel's famous 1974 article "What Is It Like to Be a Bat?" (reprinted in Nagel 1991, 165–80). Nagel argues that "the fact that an organism has conscious experience *at all* means, basically, that there is something it is like to *be* that organism" (166). He further explains that "what it is *like*," as he uses the term, "does not mean 'what (in our experience) it *resembles*,' but rather 'how it is for the subject himself'" (170). A bat's sonocentric experience—or for that matter, a dog's olfactocentric one—is so different from the oculocentric experience of human beings that we will never be able to literally feel, or entirely understand, "what it is like" to be a bat or a dog. The best we can do is to create metaphors and similes—or, as I would rather say, aesthetic semblances—that *allude* in some way to chiropteran or canine existence. Graham Harman rightly remarks that "allusion and allure are legitimate forms of knowledge" but also that they are necessarily partial and incomplete (Harman 2009b, 225). Likeness-in-human-terms, if it is projected imaginatively enough, may work to dislocate us from the correlationist position of understanding these other entities only in terms of their resemblance, and relationship, to ourselves. But it can never actually attain the inner being of those other entities.

Nagel therefore argues for a much stronger sense of "likeness." For him, it is not just a matter of our trying to explain what being a bat might be like in human terms; it is also, and more important, a question of what being a bat is like *for the bat itself.* Such is the project of what Ian Bogost, following up on Nagel, calls "alien phenomenology" (2012). As Nagel puts it, "the experiences of other creatures are certainly independent of the reach of an analogy with the human case. They have their own reality and their own subjectivity" (1991, 191). In affirming this, Nagel moves from the problem of access to the problem of being: from epistemology (the question of how we can know what a bat is thinking) to ontology (grasping that the bat is indeed thinking and that this thinking is an essential aspect of the bat's own being, even though we cannot hope to comprehend it). It is evidently "like something" to be a bat, but we will never be able to imagine or to state in words just what that "something" is. The point is a double one. The bat's thinking is inaccessible to us; we should not anthropomorphize the bat's experience by modeling it on our own. But we also should not claim that just because it is nonhuman, or not like us, the bat cannot have experiences at all. These are really just two sides of the same coin. We need to accept both that the bat *does* have experiences and that these experiences are radically different from ours and may have their own richness and complexity in ways that we will never be able to understand.

The bat's inner experience is inaccessible to me, but this is so in much the same way (albeit to a far greater extent) that any other person's inner experience is inaccessible to me. Indeed, even *my own* inner experience is inaccessible to me, in much the same way as are the inner experiences of others. This is because of the strange ontological status of "experience." I think that the later Wittgenstein is surprisingly relevant here—in spite of the fact that he is usually taken to be rejecting the very notion of mental states and inner (private) experiences. Wittgenstein does indeed say that the representations we make of our inner sensations are "not informative" (1953, #298) and that it is incoherent to speak of such sensations in the same ways that we speak of physical things. A toothache is not an object of perception in the way that a tooth is: You can see or touch my tooth, but you cannot see or touch my toothache. Indeed, the way that I feel a toothache *in* my tooth is vastly different from the way that I apprehend the tooth itself by touching it with my tongue or finger, or looking at it in the mirror, or even knowing its place through proprioception.

This line of argument has often been used, in post-Wittgensteinian analytic philosophy, to deny the existence, or the meaningfulness, of "qualia" or inner sensations altogether. But Wittgenstein himself does not do this; rather, he explicitly warns us against denying or discounting the reality of inner experience on such a basis: "Just try—in a real case—to doubt someone else's fear or pain!" (1953, #303). After all, he asks, "what greater difference could there be" than that between "pain-behaviour with pain and pain-behaviour without pain?" (#304). Inner sensation, Wittgenstein concludes, is "not a Something, but not a Nothing either!" (#304). What he means by this is that first-person experience cannot possibly be a matter of third-person, objective knowledge. First-person experience is not a Something, because—in contrast to the behavior that expresses it—it cannot be pointed to, or isolated by an observer, or made subject to scientific experimentation. But since this inner sensation, or first-person experience, is "not a Nothing either," it also cannot be eliminated or dismissed as meaningless.

This is why it is wrong to regard Wittgenstein as a behaviorist or an anti-internalist—although he has most commonly been interpreted this way. Thus Daniel Dennett conceives that he is completing the Wittgensteinian revolution in philosophy by striving to "extirpate" the very notion of "qualia that hide forever from objective science in the subjective inner sancta of our minds" (1988). Dennett takes the final reductionist step that Wittgenstein himself refuses to take—and he seems unable to understand Wittgenstein's refusal. Indeed, Dennett goes so far as to accuse Wittgenstein of trying "to hedge his bets" with the escape clause that inner sensation is "not a Nothing either." In moving toward a full-fledged eliminativism, however, Dennett throws out the baby with the bathwater. He destroys Wittgenstein's very point in the act of trying to extend it.

Wittgenstein's critique in the *Philosophical Investigations* is in fact directed as much against the functionalism and scientism that Dennett so uncritically embraces as it is against the old idealist metaphysics of the likes of, say, F. H. Bradley. Where idealism seeks to transform qualia into objectifiable facts, scientism seeks to eliminate qualia altogether on the ground that they cannot be transformed into objectifiable facts. But Wittgenstein opposes both of these moves for the same reason. He argues that not everything in the world is a matter of fact. That is to say, he explicitly contradicts the claim, from his own earlier *Tractatus*, that "the world is all that is the case" and that "the world divides into facts" that are entirely separate from one another (Wittgenstein 1922/1961, secs. 1 and 1.2). The point of Wittgenstein's later thought in the *Philosophical Investigations* is precisely to grasp the peculiar, yet ontologically positive, status of nonthings or nonfacts (such as qualia or inner sensations). And this can only be done by disabusing us of the notion either that such experiences are "facts" like all the others or that they can be "explained away" by reduction to facts. Wittgenstein thus resists the imperialistic pretensions of global idealism and global scientism alike, both of which wrongly seek to encompass everything within their own theoretical constructions.

Wittgenstein further develops his point about inner sensations in a deliberately paradoxical formulation: "I can know what someone else is thinking, not what I am thinking" (1953, II xi #315). Since I *have* feelings such as fear and pain, it is either redundant or misleading to say that I *know* I have them. The use of the word "know" in such a case implies a confusion, for there is really no epistemological issue here at all. I do not need to "know" what I am thinking in order to think it. If I am in pain, I do not need to provide grounds for proving to myself that I am so. My being in pain is therefore not a matter of "justified true belief." It is a kind of category error to think that my actual experience of fear or pain is somehow dependent on the question of how I have "access" to it or how I am able to *know* that I am experiencing it. On the other hand, I *can* rightly say that I know what you are thinking, for here I *am* able to cite grounds in order to justify my belief. Perhaps I know what you are thinking because you have told me; perhaps I gather it from your facial expression or from the way that you are acting (laughing uproariously or doubling over in pain). Of course, I may in fact be mistaken as to what you are thinking; indeed, you may be acting with the deliberate aim of deceiving me. But these sorts of errors can always be cleared up, at least in principle, through additional empirical evidence.

When it comes to my own case, the question of knowledge plays out in much the same way. I cannot be directly mistaken about being in pain. However, I *can* deceive myself about my own mental state: recent psychological experiments suggest that this happens more often than not. In this way, I might not *know* that I am in pain. Also, I may well be in error when I try to analyze my pain in discursive terms and specify to myself just *what it is* that I am thinking and feeling. This is because, to the extent that I *do* know what I myself am thinking, I am making inferences about my own thinking from the outside, in just the same way that I make inferences about the mental states of others. In a similar vein, Thomas Metzinger notes that I can have phenomenal, conscious experience of a state—like "the pure 'suchness' of the finest shades of conscious color experience"—that "is available for attention and online motor control, but it is not available for cognition . . . it evades cognitive access in principle. It is nonconceptual content" (2004, 72–73). Thus I experience things that I cannot, in principle, *know.*

If we try to extend Wittgenstein's line of questioning to nonhuman others, then the problem is evidently one of language, since Wittgenstein is so concerned with forms of speech in particular. Nagel expresses a certain uneasiness with Wittgenstein's account, because "it depends too heavily on our language . . . But not all conscious beings are capable of language, and that leaves the difficult problem of how this view accommodates the subjectivity of *their* mental states" (1991).

However, Nagel (1991) goes on to alleviate this difficulty: "We ascribe experience to animals on the basis of their behavior, structure, and circumstances, but we are not just ascribing to them behavior, structure, and circumstances. So what are we saying? The same kind of thing we say of people when we say they have experiences, of course" (191). Also, "experience must have systematic connexions with behavior and circumstances in order for experiential qualities and experiential similarity to be real. But we need not know what these connexions are in order to ask whether experience is present in an alien thing" (191–92).

My cat does not tell me what she wants in words, as another human person would be able to do. Nonetheless, I can often rightly say that I know, from observation, what my cat is thinking (she wants dinner; she wants me to brush her; she wants to be left alone). More important, even when I cannot tell what my cat is thinking, I can at least tell that she *is* thinking. I know that the "connexions" are there, even if I don't know what they are, and I know that "experience" requires such "connexions" but also that it cannot be reduced to them. My cat's inner experiences are in no way dependent on my ability to "translate" them into my own terms, nor are they vitiated by her inability to justify them by means of predicative judgments or to articulate the "inferential relations" implied by the conceptualization of these experiences (here I am drawing on—and expressing disagreement with—Wolfendale 2009).

All this implies that language should not be accorded too privileged a place in our inferences about inner experience; much less should language be necessary in order for some sort of inner experience to exist. What David Chalmers calls the "hard problem" of consciousness (1995) indeed plays out the same way in relation to a bat, or a cat, or, for that matter—in Chalmers's notorious example—a thermostat (1997, 293ff.) as it does in relation to another human being. In the latter case, species similarity and the common ability to speak allow us to describe "what it is like" for the other person a bit more extensively, but this is only a difference of degree, not one of kind. An extreme behaviorist will deny the existence of interiority in speaking human beings as well as in nonspeaking animals and nonliving thermostats. But there is no justification for inferring interiority on the basis of linguistic behavior while at the same time refusing to make such an inference in the case of other sorts of observed behavior.

With or without language, therefore, we are observing the behavior of others (or even of ourselves) in order to infer the existence of an inner experience that, in its own right, is irreducible to observable behavior. Following Wittgenstein's suggestions, we must say that this inner experience indeed exists, but it does so in a quite particular manner. Inner mental states, such as sensations and experiences, are not reducible to discursive language for the same reason that they are not objectifiable as "facts" that can be observed directly in the third person. "What it is like to be a bat" is not a Something, for it is not specifiable as a *thing* at all. But the bat's inner experience is not a Nothing either. This means that it is indeed "like something" to be a bat, even though "what it is like" is not *a* Something. This distinction is not a mere play on words but a basic ontological condition. The mentality of a bat cannot be displayed objectively, but it also cannot simply be dismissed or explained away. A bat's experience—or a human being's, for that matter—is indubitable and incorrigible, but at the same time, it is spectral, impalpable, and incommunicable.

Indeed, this is why the very attempt to discuss subjective experience in terms of qualia, precise sensations, and the like is—as Wittgenstein suggested—not very useful. As Whitehead, for his part, continually points out, most experience is vague and indistinct. We largely confront "percepta which are vague, not to be controlled, heavy with emotion" (*PR*, 178). Primordial experience involves "a sense of influx of influence from other vaguer presences in the past, localized and yet evading local definition, such influence modifying, enhancing, inhibiting, diverting, the stream of feeling which we are receiving, unifying, enjoying, and transmitting. This is our general sense of existence, as one item among others, in an efficacious actual world" (*PR*, 178).

Or, as Whitehead puts it in an earlier passage in *Process and Reality*, "the primitive experience is emotional feeling," but "the feeling is blind and the relevance is vague" (*PR*, 163). Very few aspects of our experience are actually clear and distinct; we can only obtain "a clear-cut experience by concentrating on the abstractions of consciousness" (*MT*, 108) and ignoring or excluding everything else.

Whitehead suggests that the fatal mistake of philosophers from Descartes through Hume was to restrict themselves to such abstractions by taking "clear and distinct ideas" as their starting point. We may say much the same about analytic philosophers today who argue about qualia, for the problem with speaking of "qualia" at all—pro or con—is that by invoking them in the first place, we have already distorted them by extracting them from the Jamesian stream of consciousness in which they occur. Once we have done so, it is easy enough to take the further step that Dennett does and "prove" that they do not exist at all. In other words, Dennett's eliminativism is merely the reductio ad absurdum of the premises that he shares with his opponents. Most of our experience is already lost once it has been analyzed in detail and divided into discrete parts. All these discussions in the philosophy of mind miss the point, because mentality is both far more diffuse and far more widespread than these thinkers realize. Such, at least, is Whitehead's version of the claim that mentality is neither a Something nor a Nothing.

I think that Galen Strawson's argument for panpsychism (2006) makes the most sense if it is read in light of these considerations. Strawson argues that mentality of some sort—whether we call it "experience, 'consciousness,' conscious experience, 'phenomenology,' experiential 'what-it's-likeness,' feeling, sensation, explicit conscious thought"—is "the phenomenon whose existence is more certain than the existence of anything else" (3). Everything that we know about the world, and everything that we do in fact experience, is dependent on the prior condition that we are able to *have experiences* in the first place. The mental, for Strawson, is therefore not something that we can point to: we have already preassumed it, even before we look for it explicitly. Therefore, he says, we must reject "the view—the faith—that the nature or essence of all concrete reality can in principle be fully captured in the terms of *physics*" (4). Indeed, according to Strawson, the *only* way to explain "the nature or essence of experience" in "the terms of physics" is to explain it away, eliminating it almost by definition (4). Reductionists like Dennett end up trying to "deny the existence of experience altogether"—a move that Strawson regards as absurd and self-refuting (7).

In insisting that we are surer of our own conscious experience than of anything else, Strawson knowingly echoes the Cartesian cogito. But he gets rid of the dualism and the reification that have always been seen as the most problematic parts of Descartes's argument. For Strawson, "experiential phenomena" are real in their own right (2006, 4), and there cannot be an experience without an experiencer. But at the same time, Strawson makes no particular claim about the nature of the "I" that thinks, and he certainly does not pronounce himself to be a "thinking *thing.*" Whereas Descartes posited mind as entirely separate from matter or extension, Strawson makes precisely the opposite move. Given the evident reality of the mental, together with a basic commitment to what he calls "real physicalism," he says that we must reject the common assumption that "the physical, in itself, is an essentially and wholly non-experiential phenomenon" (11). If we reject dualism and supernaturalism, then mentality itself must be entirely physical.

This might seem to be altogether reasonable once we have accepted—as Whitehead already urged us to do nearly a century ago and as many speculative realists and new materialists now assert—that matter is not inert and passive but immanently active, productive, and formative. However, this is not quite Strawson's claim, for he is not arguing for the vibrancy of matter on the basis of quantum theory, as Whitehead did and as Karen Barad currently does (2007); nor is he arguing for it on the basis of the new sciences of complexity and emergence, as Jane Bennett (2010), Manuel Delanda (2002), and other new materialists tend to do. Rather, Strawson's position is radically anti–systems theory and antiemergentist. He rejects the idea that anything nontrivial can emerge on a higher level that was not already present in and linearly caused by microconstituents at a lower level. Wetness can arise from the agglomeration of water molecules that are not in themselves wet; this is something that physics has no trouble explaining (Strawson 2006, 13–14). And although we do not know for sure how life originally came out of nonlife, we are able at least to develop plausible and coherent physicochemical scenarios about how it might have happened. The emergence of life—which seemed so mysterious to the nineteenth-century vitalists—does not trouble us *metaphysically* any longer. But Strawson insists that "one cannot draw a parallel between the perceived problem of life and the perceived problem of experience in this way, arguing that the second problem will dissolve just as the first did, unless one considers life completely apart from experience" (2006, 20).

According to Strawson, physics cannot even begin to explain how sentience could arise out of some initially nonsentient matter. Even if we discover the neural correlates of consciousness, that holy grail of contemporary neuroscience, this will not tell us anything about how and why inner experience is materially *possible* in the first place.

Strawson's rejection of what he calls *brute emergence* (2006, 18) rests on an unquestioned scientific reductionism, or on what Sam Coleman calls *smallism*: "the view that all facts are determined by facts about the smallest things, those that exist at the lowest level of ontology" (2006, 40). This is a position that most new materialists, and noneliminativist speculative realists, would never accept. Yet I think that we would do well to entertain Strawson's position to a certain extent, if only because it offers some resistance to our facile habit of using things like "quantum indeterminacy" and "higher-level emergence" like magic wands in order to account for whatever it is that we do not actually know how to explain. As Strawson puts it, "it is built into the heart of the notion of emergence that emergence cannot be brute in the sense of there being absolutely no reason in the nature of things why the emerging thing is as it is (so that it is unintelligible even to God)" (2006, 18). Of course, Quentin Meillassoux, with his notion of *the necessity of contingency* (2008, 65 and 71), maintains precisely this. Radical or brute emergence reaches the point of its reductio ad absurdum in Meillassoux's claim that life and sentience both arose miraculously, by pure contingency, out of a previously dead and inert universe (see Harman 2011b, 182–87).

Meillassoux in fact argues for "*the origin of pure novelty*" out of nothing (Harman 2011b, 179). But if we are to maintain—as Meillassoux emphatically does not—some version of the principle of sufficient reason, or of

Whitehead's ontological principle, then we must accept that novelty cannot emerge ex nihilo. Whitehead indeed says that creativity, or "the principle of *novelty*," is "the universal of universals characterizing ultimate matter of fact" (*PR*, 21), but he also insists that novelty is only possible on the basis of, and in response to, "stubborn fact which cannot be evaded" (*PR*, 43). Newness always depends on something prior. It is a bit like the way a DJ creates new music by sampling and remixing already-existing tracks. A similar logic leads to Strawson's insistence that sentience must already have been present, at least potentially, from the very beginning.

What is most interesting about Strawson's argument is how it leads him into a paradoxical tension, or a double bind. Strawson, like most analytic philosophers, is a scientific reductionist, yet he maintains that subjective experience is irreducible. He insists that everything is "physical" and reducible to its ultimate microcomponents and that mentality is as real, and therefore as "physical," as anything else. Yet Strawson also asserts that mentality is entirely inaccessible to scientific explanation. The very phenomenon of being able to have experiences—the phenomenon that alone makes objective, third-person knowledge possible in the first place—cannot itself be accounted for in science's objective, third-person terms. There is no way to bridge the gap between first-person and third-person perspectives.

Strawson refuses to alleviate this tension by adopting any of the usual philosophical dodges (dualism, emergentism, and eliminativism). Instead, he adopts the ontological postulate that mentality must *already* be an aspect, or a basic quality, of everything that exists. This is why "experience" cannot be limited to human beings, or even to living things in general. Panpsychism is the necessary consequence of respecting the *self-evidence* of phenomenal experience without trying either to hypostasize it or to extirpate it. Thought is not a specifiable, separable Something, but neither is it a mere vacancy, a Nothing. It is rather the inner, hidden dimension of everything. "All physical stuff is energy, in one form or another," Strawson says, "and all energy, I trow, is an experience-involving phenomenon" (2006, 25).

In this regard, Strawson's position is not far from Whitehead's. In discussing how his own philosophy of process (or of "organism") relates to the discoveries of twentieth-century science, Whitehead writes, "If we substitute the term 'energy' for the concept of a quantitative emotional intensity, and the term 'form of energy' for the concept of 'specific state of feeling,' and remember that in physics 'vector' means definite transmission from elsewhere, we see that this metaphysical description of the simplest elements in the constitution of actual entities agrees absolutely with the general principles according to which the notions of modern physics are framed" (*PR*, 116).

Whitehead adds that "direct perception [can] be conceived as the transference of throbs of emotional energy, clothed in the specific forms provided by sensa" (*PR*, 116). In this way, Whitehead, like Strawson, locates the coordinates of "experience" entirely within the natural world described to us by physics, even though such experience cannot itself be accounted for by physics. This is why subjective consciousness is spectral and unqualifiable but nonetheless entirely actual.

How is this possible? The next step in the argument is taken by Coleman, who radicalizes Nagel's formulation in the "Bat" essay. Nagel himself proposes the "what is it like" question as a kind of test: a way of determining whether or not an entity is conscious. It is evidently "like something" to be a bat, but for Nagel, it might well not be like anything at all to be a rock. Coleman, however, transforms Nagel's epistemological criterion into a foundational ontological principle. Coleman argues that "absolute what-it-is-likeness" not only applies to living things in particular; rather, it must lie "at the heart of ontology" (2009, 97). Following Bertrand Russell and Arthur Eddington, Coleman suggests that "the concepts of physics only express the extrinsic natures of the items they refer to . . . The question of their intrinsic nature is left unanswered by the theory, with its purely formal description of micro ontology" (2006, 52).

That is to say, contemporary physics—no less than the physics of Lucretius—only "tells us what an atom looks like to others"; it describes an atom in terms of its extrinsic, relational qualities. The study of these relations is what physical science is all about. But neither Lucretian, nor Newtonian, nor modern (relativistic and quantum) physics has ever pretended to tell us what an atom actually *is*, intrinsically, for itself. And this is the gap that panpsychism today seeks to fill—just as Leibniz sought to fill a similar gap in the physics of Newton. Coleman claims, therefore, that "the *essence* of the physical . . . is experiential"; all the causal interactions tracked by physics must necessarily involve, as well, "the doings of intrinsically experiential existents: causality as described by physics, as currently conceived, captures the *structure* of these goings on, but leaves out the real loci of causal power" (2006, 52).

In other words, physical science gives us true knowledge of the world, but this knowledge is exclusively external, structural, and relational. Physics can help me know what someone else is thinking, but it is powerless to explain what I am thinking. And the most hard-edged contemporary philosophy of science indeed insists on this distinction. For James Ladyman and his collaborators, the lesson of contemporary physics is that "there are no things; structure is all there is" (Ladyman, Ross, Spurrett, and Collier 2007, 130). Physical science can only describe relational properties. Ladyman and colleagues tell us that we must "give up the attempt to learn about the nature of unobservable entities from science" (92). They conclude that, since "intrinsic natures" are not known to science, they simply do not exist. As far as Ladyman is concerned, nothing has an irreducible inside; to posit one is to make an illegitimate inference as a result of what they scornfully describe as "prioritizing armchair intuitions about the nature of the universe over scientific discoveries" (10). In Ladyman's vision, physical science is exclusively relational; anything not determined by these relations must be eliminated.

Anyone who has followed recent discussions in speculative realism is likely to be aware of Graham Harman's critique of Ladyman and Ross (Harman 2010). But Harman's is only one of many voices to have found their sort of "radical relationism" untenable and to insist instead that entities *must* have intrinsic natures of some sort. William Seager summarizes various forms of what he calls the "intrinsic nature" argument and claims that without it one cannot offer anything like an adequate treatment of the problem of consciousness—much less maintain panpsychism: "We are forced to postulate an intrinsic ground for the relational, structural, or mathematical properties of which physics informs us—even if physics itself cannot provide this ground" (2006, 135). Seager and Harman alike insist, rightly, that entities must have something like intrinsic properties, because relations cannot exist without relata (Seager 2006, 140; Harman 2010, 786). Therefore, as Harman puts it, "the world swarms with individuals" (2010, 788). Whitehead, for his part, says much the same thing: "The ultimate metaphysical truth is atomism. The creatures are atomic" (*PR*, 36). If we are to account for this irreducible "plurality of actual entities" (*PR*, 18) and if we are to take seriously Coleman's demand that actually existing things (from neutrinos through houses and trees and on to galaxies) should be understood intrinsically, as "real loci of causal power," then the crucial ontological questions are the following: How we are to identify these individuals, or ultimate relata? In just what does a thing's intrinsic nature consist?

The answer, I believe, can only be that all entities have insides as well as outsides, or first-person experiences as well as observable, third-person properties. A thing's external qualities are objectively describable, but its interiority is neither a Something nor a Nothing. As Whitehead puts it, "In the analysis of actuality the antithesis between publicity and privacy obtrudes itself at every stage. There are elements only to be understood by reference to what is beyond the fact in question; and there are elements expressive of the immediate, private, personal, individuality of the fact in question. The former elements express the publicity of the world; the latter elements express the privacy of the individual" (*PR*, 289).

Everything in the universe is both public and private. A neutrino is extremely difficult to detect, for it is only affected by the weak nuclear force, and even then, its presence can only be inferred indirectly through the evidence of its rare interactions with atomic nuclei. Nonetheless, this is enough to define the neutrino as an interactional and relational entity, or what Whitehead calls a "public datum" (*PR*, 290). The neutrino cannot exist in the first place apart from the fluctuations of the quantum fields within which it is so elusively active. At the same time, we must also conceive of the privacy of the neutrino—its status as an "unobservable entity" with its own intrinsic experiencings, strange as that might seem—for it is indeed "like something" to be a neutrino.

Harman claims that all objects are "withdrawn" from access. As far as I can tell, this withdrawal is nothing more (but nothing less) than the "what-is-it-likeness," or private interior, of a thing that is *also* outwardly public and available. My problem with Harman is that he seems to underestimate this latter aspect. "Things exist not in relation," Harman writes, "but in a strange sort of vacuum from which they only partly emerge into relation" (2009b, 132). This necessarily follows, he argues, from the fact that an object can never be equated with, or reduced to, our knowledge of it: "Let's imagine that we were able to gain exhaustive knowledge of all properties of a tree (which I hold to be impossible, but never mind that for the moment). It should go without saying that even such knowledge *would not itself be a tree*. Our knowledge would not grow roots or bear fruit or shed leaves, at least not in a literal sense" (Harman 2010, 788).

The example is a good one, and Harman indeed scores a point here against the exclusively "structural realism" of Ladyman and Ross. But what leads Harman to assume in the first place that one entity's *relation* to another entity is constituted and defined by the *knowledge* that the first entity has of the second entity? Such an approach reduces ontology to epistemology. In fact, knowledge is just one particular sort of relation—and not even an especially important one at that. Most of the time, entities affect other entities blindly, without knowledge playing a part at all.

To cite one of Harman's own favorite examples, when fire burns cotton, it only encounters a few of the properties of the cotton. In the course of the conflagration, "these objects do not fully touch one another, since both harbor additional secrets inaccessible to the other, as when the faint aroma of the cotton and the foreboding sparkle of the fire remain deaf to one another's songs" (Harman 2005, 170). That is to say, the cotton has many qualities—like its texture, its aroma, and its color—that the fire never comes to "know." Harman therefore concludes that "one object never affects another directly, since the fire and the cotton both fail to exhaust one another's reality" (2005, 188), or again, "fire does not exhaust the reality of cotton by burning it" (2009b, 143).

I cannot disagree with the *epistemological* argument that Harman is making here. I find it legitimate for him to describe the interaction of fire with cotton in the same way he does the interaction of a human mind with either the fire or the cotton, and I agree with him that neither the mind nor the fire apprehends, or "knows," *all* the qualities of the cotton. Yet that is not the entire story, for there is a level of being beyond (or beneath) the epistemological one. As the cotton is burned, even those properties to which the fire is wholly insensitive are themselves also altered or destroyed—that is, fire *affects* even those aspects of the cotton that it cannot come to "know." And such is the case with all interactions among entities, when one thing affects, or is affected by, another. So while I agree with Harman that the encounter between fire and cotton does indeed involve a sort of limited knowledge, I do not think that this dimension of the encounter is in any sense definitive.

Whitehead reminds us that the inner and outer, or private and public, aspects of an entity always go together: "There are no concrete facts which are merely public, or merely private. The distinction between publicity and privacy is a distinction of reason, and is not a distinction between mutually exclusive concrete facts" (*PR*, 290). Whitehead also makes this "distinction of reason" between public and private in temporal terms. Each actual occasion occupies a particular position within the flow of time, for it is causally dependent on the other occasions in its light cone that have preceded it. However, "contemporary events . . . happen in causal independence of each other . . . The vast causal independence of contemporary occasions is the preservative of the elbow-room within the Universe. It provides each actuality with a welcome environment for irre-sponsibility" (*AI*, 195). In the thick duration of its coming-to-pass, each actual entity enjoys the freedom of its own inner experience. It *feels* in a way that is scarcely expressible. The "withdrawal" of objects can have no other meaning. At the same time, each actual entity is open to causal influences: it has been shaped by the influence of other entities that preceded it, and it will itself go on to exert causal influence on other entities that succeed it. In this way, grounded in the past and reaching toward the future, every actual entity has an immense capacity to affect and to be affected: this is what defines its outward, public aspect.

In this sense, relationalism is true. Harman is not wrong to insist that no entity is fully determined or entirely defined by its relations. As Whitehead puts it, "there is nothing in the real world which is merely an inert fact" (*PR*, 310). But Harman's claim is only one half of the story, for at the same time, it is equally the case that no entity is altogether free from the web of influences and affections, extending thorough time, that are its very conditions of existence: "All origination is private. But what has been thus originated, publically pervades the world" (*PR*, 310). This is a situation that can be read in both directions. As the Stoics observed so long ago, I am inwardly free and outwardly in chains. But I might just as well say that I am inwardly isolated and imprisoned while outwardly able to make affiliations and pursue enlivening relations. Panpsychism is the recognition that this doubleness of privacy and relationality is not just a human predicament but the condition of all entities in the universe.

6 NONCORRELATIONAL THOUGHT

THE STATUS OF *THOUGHT* remains a vexing problem for speculative realism. The speculative realists all reject the familiar Kantian and phenomenological "image of thought" (to use the felicitous phrase from Deleuze 1994, 129–67) that assumes an essential bond between thinking and its object, "the primordial interplay of human and world" (Harman 2011b, 8). For Kant, of course, these poles can never be separated: "Thoughts without content are empty; intuitions without concepts are blind" (1998, 193, B75/ A51). This means that concepts and intuitions (sensory impressions) must always go together; trying to have one without the other will only lead to error and confusion. For phenomenology, similarly, the "subject" is "destined to the world" (Merleau-Ponty 2002, xii); whenever I think, "I aim at and perceive a world" (xvii). This is precisely the correlation that speculative realism seeks to undo. But what happens when we do separate the two poles of the correlation? What remains of thought when we consider the world-without-us (Thacker 2011, 5–6) or "the autonomous reality of beings outside human thought" (Harman 2011b, 8)?

Quentin Meillassoux traces correlationism back, before Kant, to Berkeley's insistence that esse est percipi (to be is to be perceived). Berkeley, Meillassoux says, is the true "inventor of the argument of the correlationist circle" (2012, 6). As Brassier also points out, it is Berkeley who first makes the fatal slip "from the indubitable premise that 'One cannot think or perceive something without thinking or perceiving it'" to "the dubious conclusion that 'Things cannot exist without being thought or perceived'" ("Concepts and Objects," in Bryant, Srnicek, and Harman 2010, 57). Correlationism arises out of a surreptitious and sophistical inflation of the powers of thought. For Meillassoux, the only way out of this sophism is to find a way to paradoxically "think that which is, independently of *all* thought, of *all* subjectivity," including my own (Meillassoux 2012, 5).

Of course, very few correlationists actually follow Berkeley in altogether denying the existence of material things and of a world that subsists outside of thought. Most correlationists even concede that the outside world that we encounter must be understood as coming before us and preceding our very ability to think it. Thus Husserl claims to return, not to consciousness, but to "things themselves." And Merleau-Ponty, underlining the embodied nature of all experience, insists that "the world is there before any possible analysis of mine" (2002, x). Phenomenological reflection, he says, "is absolutely distinct from the idealist return to consciousness" (x).

But Meillassoux points out that this is not a sufficient alibi. The correlationist is happy to concede the world's precedence over us—except that "he will simply add . . . something like a simple codicil": the proviso that this anteriority is itself a distinction *for us*, for "a world is meaningful only as given-to-a-living (or thinking)-being" (Meillassoux 2008, 13, 15). More generally, even when correlationism *does* posit some sort of "exteriority" to thought—the Kantian thing in itself, the phenomenological intentional object, or the Lacanian Real—this exteriority still remains "relative to us . . . this space of exteriority is merely the space of what faces us, of what exists only as a correlate of our own existence" (7). For correlationism, the very being of the world inheres in its "givenness" to us (14–15). In the words of Merleau-Ponty, the subject "has to recognize, as having priority over its own operations, the world which is given to the subject because the subject is given to himself" (2002, xi). This formulation takes away human precedence with the one hand (since the world comes before the subject) only to give it back with the other (since this priority is itself "given to the subject"). As long as "givenness" retains its primacy, Meillassoux says, we are still enrolled in "the camp of Berkeley himself" (2012, 6).

What is more, this positing of the world as always already "given" to us also entails a movement of self-reflexive interiority. Correlationism implies not just a certain relation of thought to the world but also a fundamental relation of thought to itself. A thought that is correlated to objects will also take itself as an object. Thinking is therefore necessarily reflexive. Thus Kant insists that the transcendental "*I think* must *be able* to accompany all my representations" (1998, 246, B131): whenever I think of something, I must simultaneously be able to affirm my very act of thinking it. For Merleau-Ponty, similarly, "unreflective experience" must itself be reflected on, and such "reflection cannot be unaware of itself as an event" (2002, xi). Or as Vivian Sobchack puts it, in her phenomenology of the cinema, "experience comes to description in acts of reflection: consciousness turning reflexively on itself to become conscious of consciousness" (1992, xvii). Intentionality is always doubled or supplemented by self-reflexivity. We cannot truly reach out to the world, because we cannot escape from ourselves.

This is what makes it paradoxical to try to think about a "thing 'in itself,' i.e. independently of its relation to me" (Meillassoux 2008, 1). Berkeley's claim that I cannot think anything outside of my thought is a sophism, but it is one that has deep roots in our habits of thought. As Meillassoux puts it, "the materialist seems always to commit a 'pragmatic contradiction' when he claims to know a reality independent of his thought, since the reality of which he speaks is precisely that which is given him to think" (2012, 1). And that is why, as Harman says, "Meillassoux holds that correlationism must be radicalized from within, not dismissed from the outside" (2009b, 164). In order to think things apart from their relationship to me, I must deprive myself of the very coordinates that orient my thought in the first place. This is why there is no direct and simple way to argue for realism. Samuel Johnson was right in his commonsense realism, and Berkeley was wrong in his subjective idealism. But Johnson's famous act of kicking a rock does not succeed in refuting Berkeley.

For Meillassoux, then, thought must push to extremes in order to find a way to "*escape from itself.*" It is only by violating its own grounding assumptions that thought can hope to "accede to a world not yet affected by the modes of apprehension of our subjectivity" (Meillassoux 2012, 2). The paradoxical task of speculative realism is to undo the conditions that are imposed on thought by the very nature of thought itself. We must disengage ourselves from our own frame of reference, which is to say from the very grids of intelligibility—the Kantian "pure concepts of the understanding"—that we take for granted and that we have always already applied to things in the very act of perceiving them.

The inherent difficulty (or even absurdity) of this task explains why any new realism must be *speculative.* We need to subtract our own prejudices and presuppositions from any account we give of the world. And we need to create a new image of thought: one that is no longer modeled on, or limited to, anthropocentric parameters. Speculation must therefore be both *subtractive* (in the manner of Alain Badiou) and *additive* (in the manner of Gilles Deleuze). And if such speculation succeeds, then it will necessarily give us, as Meillassoux puts it, "the legitimate feeling of being on foreign territory—of being entirely elsewhere" (2008, 7). We must alienate ourselves from ourselves in order to look at correlationism from a noncorrelational perspective and comprehend how the world exists apart from us.

When Meillassoux first defines correlationism, he presents what seems to be a symmetrical formulation. Correlationism, he says, is "the idea according to which we only ever have access to the correlation between thinking and being, and never to either term considered apart from the other" (2008, 5). Subject and object, or more generally thought and being, are regarded by the correlationist as mutually coconstituting and codependent: "Not only does it become necessary to insist that we never grasp an object in itself, in isolation from its relation to the subject, but it also becomes necessary to maintain that we can never grasp a subject that would not always-already be related to an object" (Meillassoux 2008, 5). Described in this manner, the correlation would seem to move indifferently in either direction, from thinking to being or from being to thinking. And such is indeed the case for phenomenology, which fits Meillassoux's description more fully than any other school of modern philosophy.

However, under closer examination, Meillassoux's formulation turns out not to be symmetrical or reversible after all. Rather, he describes the correlationist movement in unidirectional terms. When thought and being are correlated, thought is always the active and relational term: the one that actually *performs* the correlation. Thinking per se is correlational insofar as it necessarily implies a "relation-to-the-world" (Meillassoux 2008, 18, 37). Indeed, thought begins with a radical double "decision": the assertion "of the essential inseparability of the act of thinking from its content" (36) and then the "absolutization" of this correlation (37). Once this double decision has been made, it is already too late: "all we ever engage with is what is given-to-thought, never an entity subsisting by itself" (36).

On the other hand, being—in contrast to thought—just *is*. This makes it the dumb and passive term in Meillassoux's account. Meillassoux takes it for granted that objects, unlike subjects, are able to stand alone. Things do not correlate on their own and do not make decisions: according to Meillassoux, they do not engage in any sort of internally generated activity at all. They merely suffer being apprehended by—and thereby correlated to—some sort of consciousness or subjectivity that seizes them from the outside. In itself, being is not given and does not speak. Thus thought always refers to being, but being in itself remains indifferent to thought. Since ancestral reality does not exist *for us*, it does not exist *in thought* at all: it is "anterior to givenness" and refuses any sort of "manifestation" whatsoever (14).

The conclusion follows that since thought is in its essence correlational, we can only escape correlationism by affirming "the pure and simple *death*, with neither consciousness nor life, without any subjectivity whatsoever, that is represented by the state of inorganic matter" (Meillassoux 2012, 6): "Absolute reality is an *entity without thought*"

(Meillassoux 2008, 36). Meillassoux tells us that we must conceive of a world that has "no subjective-psychological, egoic, sensible or vital traits whatsoever" (2012, 2).

The paradoxical task of speculative philosophy, for Meillassoux, is therefore to find a way for thought to turn back on and erase itself. Meillassoux seeks to operate a kind of dialectical reversal, by means of which "thought has become able to think a world that can dispense with thought, a world that is essentially unaffected by whether or not anyone thinks it" (2008, 116). In order to achieve this, thought must commit suicide, as it were, in order to be resurrected in an entirely new and different form. Meillassoux makes the audacious gesture of exterminating perception and sentience altogether, chasing them from all their hiding places. He mounts a "materialist struggle against every form of hypostasis of the subjective (not only of the subject in a limited sense, as consciousness, reason, freedom, but of the subject in all its modalities—will, sensation, preconscious life, etc.)" (Meillassoux 2012, 6).

The surprising result of this struggle, however, is the birth of a new kind of thought: one that "is capable of the 'absolute', capable even of producing something like 'eternal truths'" (Meillassoux 2012, 1). Such a purified, noncorrelational thought is purely rational, logical, and theoretical: a "veritable *intellectual intuition* of the absolute" (Meillassoux 2008, 82). Meillassoux boasts that there is no empirical basis whatsoever for "the 'absolutizing' capacity of thought" (2012, 1); it quite literally rests on nothing. It has no relation to the body or to any sort of experience. It has no ties to sensibility or to affect. It cannot be explained in continuist or evolutionary terms. This sort of thought arises ex nihilo, for no reason, without any prior basis, and sheerly by chance (*The Divine Inexistence*, in Harman 2011b, 175–87). As an affirmation of pure contingency, Meillassoux's intellectual intuition "says nothing as to the factual being of our world" (Meillassoux 2012, 13). For Meillassoux, thought can only escape correlation to the extent that it does not affect the world and is not affected by it.

In place of the correlation of thought and being, therefore, Meillassoux presents us with the stark dualism of an absolute thought without being and a being entirely devoid of thought. He identifies the latter with the classical picture—derived from the scientific revolution of the seventeenth and eighteenth centuries and, even before that, from the ancient atomists and Epicureans (Meillassoux 2008, 36–37; 2012, 2)—of a universe that is lifeless, mindless, and inert and that operates entirely mechanistically. This also means that Meillassoux empties the world of what Kant called "sensible intuition": that is, of anything and everything that is experienced phenomenally and that is discovered through the body and the senses.

In other words, Meillassoux designedly reaffirms the very condition that Alfred North Whitehead diagnosed as the basic error of modern Western thought: the "bifurcation of nature" (*CN*, 30). This is the schema according to which we radically separate sensory experience from the physical actualities that generate that experience. We divide "the perceived redness and warmth of the fire" on the one hand from "the agitated molecules of carbon and oxygen," the "radiant energy," and the "various functionings of the material body" on the other (32). These two descriptions are taken to belong to entirely separate registers of existence. The first is phenomenal, while the second is scientific.

Once we have divided up the world in this manner, Whitehead tells us, it matters little which side of the bifurcation we favor. Phenomenology valorizes perceptual experience while ignoring, or failing to give an adequate account of, the molecules and the photons. Reductionist scientism, on the other hand, disparages phenomenal experience as merely a "psychic addition, furnished by the perceiving mind," and not really present in "the molecules and the radiant energy which influence the mind toward that perception" (*CN*, 29–30). Both approaches fail at the task of accounting for the world in "one system of relations" (*CN*, 32), beyond all oppositions of subject and object. Both of them "indulge in brilliant feats of explaining away" important aspects of experience (*PR*, 17). Both of them ignore Whitehead's dictum—an example of anti-correlationism avant la lettre—that "no perplexity concerning the object of knowledge can be solved by saying that there is a mind knowing it" (*CN*, 28).

Meillassoux calls on mathematics and physical science in order to validate the bifurcation of nature. This is because "empirical science is today capable of producing statements about events anterior to the advent of life as well as consciousness," which are therefore not receivable within the correlationist framework (Meillassoux 2008, 9). Scientific research literally and objectively confronts us with actualities that cannot in any way be correlated with thought. Science and mathematics intimate to us "a world crammed with things and events that are not the correlates of any manifestation, a world that is not the correlate of a relation to the world" (26); Meillassoux claims that the "primary qualities" of matter measured by science are entirely nonrelational and therefore not *for us* (1). All—but only—"those aspects of the object that can be formulated in mathematical terms can be meaningfully conceived as properties of the object in itself" (3). The "mathematization of nature" performed by physical science thus allows us, as other modes of understanding do not, "to know what may be while we are not . . . What is mathematizable cannot be reduced to a correlate of thought" (115, 117).

On the other hand, according to Meillassoux, subjective apprehensions— or what Descartes and Locke called "secondary qualities"—are appearances that are not really present in the world; they are only "lyingly added" (as Nietzsche would say) to objects by our own activity in perceiving them (Meillassoux 2008, 3). Sensory qualities always involve "a relation, rather than a property inherent in the thing" (2). This means that they are inevitably correlational and epiphenomenal. Meillassoux therefore suggests that we must reject anything having to do with phenomenality, with embodiment, and with sensibility and affect. Everything belonging to "perception and sensation" must be removed; we are left only with those elements that are reducible "to a formula or to digitization" (3).

Such a distinction—between properties that belong to an object absolutely and those that are only explained by what Whitehead called "psychic additions" (*CN*, 29)—is still all too commonly made today, even by thinkers who have rejected the outdated terminology of "primary" and "secondary" qualities. Indeed, this sort of distinction is so often taken for granted that it is hard to realize just how strange and arbitrary it is. For example, the speculative realist philosopher Levi Bryant takes up just such a position—despite the fact that he is much closer to Harman's object-oriented ontology than he is to Meillassoux's apparent scientism. Bryant argues that "qualities like the beauty of sunsets and the qualities of rainbows are exo-qualities: they *only* arise in relations. Take away neurological systems with particular biological (and cultural) imperatives, and there are no *beautiful* sunsets. There are just waves of electromagnetism proliferating throughout the world. Take away organisms capable of perceiving colors and there are no rainbows." To the contrary, Bryant says, what he calls "endo-qualities" are "qualities of the things *themselves*"; any such quality exists independently, for it is "there regardless of whether or not anything *relates* to it" (Bryant 2013).

Now, it is true that so-called secondary qualities, like the colors of a rainbow, need to be detected by our eyes or by some other sort of perceptual apparatus. But this is an epistemological matter, not an ontological one. In fact, the same is equally true for the quantifiable, supposedly primary qualities of things in themselves, like their mass and volume; these too cannot be detected and specified without the help of some measuring apparatus. Not possessing a scale or a ruler (or equivalent scientific instruments) puts me in the same quandary as not possessing the cones for color vision in my eyes. For this reason, distinctions between primary and secondary qualities (or between endo-qualities and exo-qualities) cannot serve the purpose that Meillassoux and Bryant would like them to. (The question of beauty is quite different from that of secondary qualities like colors; I will take it up in what follows.)

In other words, I run into the same problem of *access* with primary qualities (or endo-qualities) as I do with secondary qualities (or exo-qualities). Whether I am dealing with quantifiable properties like volume, mass, and wavelength or with "qualitative" ones like color, I am still stuck within the correlationist circle. Epistemologically speaking, I can never eliminate my reliance on the mediating practices of measurement and perception.

Mechanical and technological devices might well give me different results from those I get using my bodily senses alone. But this applies to secondary, as much as to primary, qualities: the digital video camera is as transformative a technical device as is a spectroscope. In all cases, as Bruno Latour puts it, "there are no equivalents, only translations" (1988, 162).

This means that in the case of so-called primary qualities (endoqualities) and secondary qualities (exo-qualities) alike, I cannot avoid making human-centered judgments, for I cannot simply transcend my own correlational framework. My apprehension of mass is no less "relational" than my apprehension of color. In both cases, I am unable to access the actual properties of objects *in themselves*. It makes no sense, therefore, to divide these properties into classes (primary and secondary) and to judge that one class is more authentic, or intrinsic to things in themselves, than the other. If we reject solipsism, then we must say—as Kant already argued—that our perceptions are in fact *responding to*, and *affected by*, the actual properties of actual objects. But we do not have unmediated access to these properties, and this is equally the case for those we call "primary" and "secondary."

I am therefore compelled to agree with Graham Harman that quantifiable or digitizable "primary" qualities must be placed in the same category as sensory "secondary" ones (Harman 2011b, 152). In both instances, our knowledge is correlational; in both cases, we cannot equate what we know (partially and extrinsically) about things with the actual being of the things themselves. However, my formulation of this point is somewhat different from Harman's. Whereas he says that no amount of "information" about a thing can "replicate" or "add up to" that thing (147–48), I find it more accurate to say that no amount of information can ever *exhaust* the thing. Harman claims that our perception of the moon is "a more or less accurate model, composed of a vastly simplified range of features" (148). Like all models, our picture of the moon is an abstraction that leaves many things out. There is never enough information: even "the exhaustive reams of information available to almighty God" (148) would not be enough to fully grasp the moon itself.

Now, I accept this up to a point. But overall, I do not think that my perception of the moon can be equated with a mental "model" of it. I am uneasy with this claim for the same reason that I am uneasy with Thomas Metzinger's argument that consciousness is essentially representational (Metzinger 2004, 15ff. and passim) and that conscious perception is really just a sort of virtual-reality simulation (312ff. and passim). For the notion of a model, or a simulation, tends to overly simplify what is a much more complicated process. Rather than assuming a more or less adequate correspondence between an internal mental model and an outside state of affairs to which that model strives to correspond, we would do better to consider perception as a nonrepresentational process of continual feedback, response, and adjustment.

My prehension (to use Whitehead's term) of the moon is not a model or a representation of the moon but a kind of contact-at-a-distance. It cannot rightly be described, as the old empiricists would have done, as an impression (or bundle of impressions) that is passively received by, or inscribed on, my mind. But it also cannot rightly be described in phenomenological terms as a mental action of taking the moon as the "intentional object" of my thought. Neither is adequate to describe the way that the actual moon really and truly *affects* me. Something within me changes when I see the moon: my encounter with it produces a *difference* within me. But this difference cannot be correlated with any actual properties of the moon itself. My contact with the moon is an ongoing process of adjustment or of Latourian "translation." This is why my encounter with the moon runs deeper than anything I can *know* about it. As Whitehead puts it, in such an encounter, the prehending entity is involved in "'feeling' the many data" that it receives from other entities (*PR*, 40). This "feeling" of "data" may involve, but it cannot be *reduced to*, a matter of knowledge or cognition. I think, therefore, that Harman gives too much weight to the informational and epistemological limits of contact between entities but that, on the other hand, he does not give sufficient ontological weight to what he interestingly describes as "vicarious causation" (2007b) or "indirect causation" (2011a, 69–81).

In any case, and despite these differences of nuance, I agree with Harman that "primary qualities" cannot provide us with absolute, extra-correlational access to things in the way that Meillassoux claims. And I follow Harman in seeing Meillassoux's stance as a version of what Harman calls *epistemism*, or the dubious assertion that "there is a privileged mathematical or scientific access to reality" (2012b). Harman rightly notes that the dispute as to whether mathematics and science allow us a kind of noncorrelational access to reality is "the most important fault line running through speculative realism" today (2012b). It divides Meillassoux and Brassier, on the one side, from Harman, Grant, and myself, on the other.

Some additional remarks may be in order regarding Meillassoux's recourse to mathematics. Meillassoux argues at great length for the "absolutizing" power of mathematics and logic: their capacity to work in a formal manner with "meaningless signs" devoid of meaning or reference. He claims that by so doing, mathematics and logic do indeed "give us the means to identity the properties of a world that is radically independent of thought" (Meillassoux 2012, 18ff.). But Alexander Galloway suggests that mathematics is not as exempt from the logic of correlationism as Meillassoux would like to believe. Today, at least, the empty formalism of mathematics cannot be seen as an objective, neutral, and indifferent process, for the mathematical formalization of all aspects of our world is a crucial and indispensable component of our "post-Fordist (that is computerized) modernity" (Galloway 2012, 4:11). Today, "under post-Fordism qualities derived from math *would most certainly be socially and subjectively determined*" (4:12). What Meillassoux wants to claim as being beyond the correlation is, in fact, the central mechanism of production and control in our current mode of production. It is mathematization, more than anything else, that today enforces and ensures the correlation between the physical world and our desires—or more accurately, the desires of Capital.

Galloway therefore suggests that mathematics, computation, and algorithmic procedures play the same role for Meillassoux—and also for

Badiou and for the late Lacan—that language played for Lévi-Strauss, Barthes, Derrida, the early Foucault, and the early Lacan. Like so many thinkers before him, Meillassoux models his ontology on the prevailing mode of production or of sociotechnological order. As Galloway puts it, "in the age of the steam engine, man is a dynamo and society a vast machine that may be tamed or exploited. And now, in the age of the algorithm, it is pure math that makes claims about the world and extracts value from it" (Galloway 2012, 4:12). From this point of view, mathematization does not exceed the correlation of thought and being but remains—no less than language—firmly ensconced within it.

The reductionist dismissal of subjective and phenomenal qualities is actually made more rigorously by Ray Brassier than it is by Meillassoux. Brassier, much like Meillassoux, rejects the privilege that traditional philosophy has accorded to subjectivity, experience, and thought. And Brassier, again like Meillassoux, turns to physical science as a way to escape from correlationism. Brassier also reconceptualizes the bifurcation of nature along the lines of Wilfrid Sellars's distinction between the "manifest image" derived from human self-conceptions, and the "scientific image," which "can be distilled from various scientific discourses" (Brassier 2007, 3). It is not possible, Brassier says, to simply eliminate the delusive manifest image, leaving us only with the true scientific one (9ff.). But he strongly insists that once science rids us of our "psychological need for stories," we are left with a world that is "not *for* anything" and not "comprehensible in narrative terms" (Brassier 2011).

Brassier argues, against all forms of correlationism, that thought never coincides with its intentional content. Thinking involves intentionality, or *aboutness*, but our thoughts never actually correspond with the things that they are about. Indeed, Brassier insists that "thought is not guaranteed access to being; being is not inherently thinkable"; we live in "a world that is not designed to be intelligible and is not originarily infused with meaning" ("Concepts and Objects," in Bryant et al. 2010, 47). Consequently, there is always a "gap," or a "discrepancy," between "what our concept of the object is and what the object is in itself" (55).

This very gap or discrepancy is what grounds Brassier's scientism and eliminativism. For Brassier, neither science nor metaphysics can overcome the noncoincidence between things themselves and the ways that these things are represented in our thought. But Brassier adds that even philosophies that affirm this fundamental noncoincidence—such as that, most notably, of Deleuze—remain idealist and correlationist to the extent that they posit this originary difference as a difference *for thought* itself (Brassier 2007, 203). Against this, Brassier's "transcendental realism" (118) makes the case that the inevitable difference between a concept and that to which it refers can itself never be conceptualized; this difference always remains extraconceptual.

The fundamental difference between science and metaphysics, Brassier argues, is that for science, "the reality of the object determines the meaning of its conception," whereas metaphysics assumes the reverse (in Bryant et al. 2010, 55). The difference between reality and how it is thought "is at once determining for thought and irreducible to thinking" (Brassier 2007, 203). But science, unlike metaphysics, actually "allows the discrepancy between that reality and the way in which it is conceptually circumscribed to be measured" (in Bryant et al. 2010, 55). With this distinction, Brassier defends science—of affirms a version of epistemism—in such a way that avoids Meillassoux's claim to attain absolute knowledge directly through quantitative measurements. For Brassier, we cannot directly measure things themselves, as they exist apart from us, but we can measure, at least indirectly, the inadequacy of our concepts with regard to the things to which they are supposed to refer.

Brassier's major argument, therefore, is not just that the world is meaningless. More crucially, he argues that through physical science "it is possible to *understand* the meaninglessness of existence" (Brassier 2011). Or, to put the point even more strongly, just as science measures the discrepancy between things and our conceptions of them without conceptualizing the discrepancy itself, so science is able to understand the meaninglessness of existence without turning this meaningless (as existentialism, for instance, does) into yet another source of meaning. For

Brassier, "this capacity to understand meaning as a regional or *bounded* phenomenon marks a fundamental progress in cognition" (2011).

In Brassier's vision, thought is increasingly compelled by the very progress of scientific knowledge to recognize its own irrelevance and impotence. Once it is no longer correlated to being, "thought becomes the locus for the identity of absolute objectivity and impersonal death" (Brassier 2007, 204). This means that scientific knowledge, achieved through thought, leads ultimately to the extinction of thought—or, more precisely, to thought's recognition of its own extinction. Not only is the philosopher mortal, but "the subject of philosophy must also recognize that he or she is *already* dead" (239; emphasis added). When "the absence of correlation" itself becomes "an object of thought," it thereby "transforms thought itself into an object" so that "extinction indexes the thought of the absence of thought" (229–30). For Brassier, the consequence of rejecting correlationism is that we come to recognize a universe that is not only irreducible to thought but fatally inimical to thought.

Meillassoux, in contrast to Brassier, only recruits positivistic science and mathematical formalization opportunistically. He does not take scientific and mathematical formalization as the last word. Indeed, I would go so far as to suggest that science and mathematics are ultimately not important to Meillassoux at all. Physical science gives him the argument that ancestral objects exist prior to any sort of manifestation for a subject. And Georg Cantor's theory of transfinites provides the basis for his demonstration (following Badiou) that the set of possible future events does not constitute a totality and therefore cannot be understood in terms of relative probabilities. But once these arguments have been established, science and mathematics no longer play a crucial role. When Meillassoux praises the way that Badiou "uses mathematics itself to effect a liberation from the limits of calculatory reason" (2008, 103), he is saying something that applies even more fully to his own philosophy.

Indeed, Meillassoux's major claim—that the "laws of nature" are entirely contingent and that at any time they "could actually change for no reason" (2008, 84)—would seem to undermine scientific rationality altogether. Science cannot work without assuming the validity of relations of cause and effect—which is to say, without some degree of confidence or faith (however attenuated) in the "principle of sufficient reason" that Meillassoux rejects (60 and passim). All this makes it evident that Meillassoux is interested neither in demystifying and naturalizing our theories of mind nor in reducing subjectivity to its ostensible microphysical causes. He rejects what he calls "naturalism," or the grounding of philosophy on a "state of science that has no more reason to be thought definitive today than it did yesterday" (Meillassoux 2012, 11).

Far more radically, Meillassoux seeks to achieve a total purgation of thought from being in order thereby to clear the way for his own absolute rationalism. He achieves the elimination of meaning by fiat, whereas Brassier sees it as the final consequence of a long process of demystification and enlightenment. In other words, Meillassoux embraces mathematization not because it helps give us scientifically valid and objective (noncorrelational) results but only because it works to get rid of sentience and meaning altogether. He values physical science not for its own sake but only because—and to the extent that—it allows us to reject the very notion of subjectivity. Science and mathematics, in other words, are tools that Meillassoux uses to get rid of phenomenology. Whereas Nietzsche feared that we were not getting rid of God because we still believed in grammar, Meillassoux fears that we are not getting rid of correlationism because we still believe in phenomenal experience.

I want to suggest that the reason both Brassier and Meillassoux reaffirm the bifurcation of nature and banish meaning and sentience from the physical universe is, paradoxically, because, in their evident epistemism, they aren't anticorrelationalist *enough*. This goes back to the asymmetry in Meillassoux's initial definition of correlationism, which I mentioned earlier. Meillassoux goes to great lengths in order to escape the correlationist demand that "we never grasp an object 'in itself', in isolation from its relation to the subject." But he fails—indeed, he never tries—to work against the reciprocal demand of correlationism that "we can never grasp a subject that would not always-already be related to an object." Indeed, Meillassoux takes this claim entirely for granted. This is why his self-proclaimed "materialism" requires the elimination of any "sensible mode of subjectivity" (Meillassoux 2012, 4). It is also why, on the other side, the only positive image of thought that he is willing to countenance is an entirely formal, abstract, and asubjective one: the "intellectual intuition of the absolute." It is almost as if, having abolished the correlational structure of Kant's first critique, Meillassoux leaves us instead with an odd epistemization of the second critique: the vision of an absolute rationality to whose imperatives mere phenomena can never fully conform.

The principal target of Meillassoux's polemic is phenomenology, the legacy of Husserl, Heidegger, and Merleau-Ponty. With its insistence on "the primordial interplay of human and world" and its refusal to recognize "the autonomous reality of beings outside human thought," phenomenology is the correlationist philosophy par excellence. Yet despite his opposition to phenomenology, Meillassoux still takes for granted, and never questions, the phenomenological assumption that perception and sentience are fundamentally and necessarily *intentional*. In phenomenology, every act of thinking is directed to an object beyond itself. A mental state always *points to* something. This remains the case regardless of whether that "something" is a thing that really exists in the world or whether it is fiction, or an abstraction, or a mental construction. No matter the situation, thought is always *about* something. It follows that thought is intrinsically a *relational* activity, and indeed a *correlational* one. The "decision" that inaugurates thought has ruled out any other possibility.

Meillassoux thus presents only a one-sided escape from correlationism. He fully explores the way that objects exist in themselves rather than just being *for us*. But apart from his arbitrary assertion of intellectual intuition, he fails to consider how thought might also subsist on its own, *in itself*, without the need for any intentionalistic "relation-to-the-world." A more thoroughgoing anticorrelationism must also explore the existence of *noncorrelational thought*: that is to say, of a sort of thought—or consciousness, or sentience, or feeling, or phenomenal experience—that is nonphenomenological insofar as it goes on without establishing relations of intentionality to anything beyond itself and even without establishing any sort of reflexive relation to itself. If we seek to liberate the world of objects from its servitude as a mere correlate of our thought, then we must also strive to liberate thought from its servitude to things, as well as to its own self-imposed grounds, reasons, and conditions of possibility. And this must be done without inflating rationality to a transcendent status. Meillassoux's "intellectual intuition of the absolute" marks the place in his schema of a possibility that he otherwise fails to explore.

This point can also be made another way. There is a curious slippage in the course of Meillassoux's analysis. He argues that any noncorrelationist philosophy must be open to "an absolute that is at once external to thought and in itself devoid of all subjectivity" (Meillassoux 2012, 2). The slippage comes in the way that Meillassoux implicitly moves from an object, or a world, that is independent of anything that *our* thought imposes on it to objects and worlds that are also devoid of thought *in themselves*. Meillassoux seems to take it for granted that thought is unique to human beings, at least on this planet. Due to "the rupture inaugurated by thought with respect to animality," he says, we are uniquely "rational beings capable of grasping the absolute truth of contingency" (*The Divine Inexistence*, in Harman 2011b, 190). Meillassoux therefore frankly defends his own *anthropocentrism* in opposition to what he describes as "an anthropomorphism that consists in the illusion of seeing in every reality (even inorganic reality) subjective traits the experience of which is in fact entirely human, merely varying their degree (an equally human act of imagination)" (2012, 5).

However, such human exceptionalism is both arbitrary and unwarranted. Meillassoux accuses antianthropocentric modern thinkers (from Diderot, through Schelling, Schopenhauer, Nietzsche, and Bergson, and to Deleuze) of being secretly anthropomorphic and of smuggling human "subjective traits" into everything in the cosmos (2012, 3). But Meillassoux plays fast and loose with this claim, since he takes it for granted that ascribing "subjective traits" to nonhuman entities means "absolutizing the subjective" (3)—that is to say, defining those entities *exhaustively* and *exclusively* in terms of such subjective traits. But this is simply wrong. As Harman points out, "even if we postulate that a rock is a perceiving entity, it would not follow that its existence consists entirely in perceiving" (2013, 24). I thus entirely concur with Harman's claim that Meillassoux's category of "subjectalism"—meant to include idealists, vitalists, and pantheists under the same rubric—does not hold up to careful scrutiny (Harman 2013, 24–25).

Moreover, in his attack on "subjectalist" claims in modern philosophy, Meillassoux never accounts for his own assumption that these traits are "in fact entirely human"—and exclusively so—in the first place. He seems to take it as obvious, and self-evident, that human thought marks a radical "rupture . . . with respect to animality." But, in fact, there are no grounds, apart from the anthropocentric prejudices of Western modernity, for asserting such a rupture between human thought and animal being. Recent biological research has amply demonstrated the sentience not just of nonhuman animals but of other kinds of organisms as well (Shaviro 2011). It is not being anthropomorphic, but simply empirically accurate to heed the ways that fruit flies make decisions (Brembs 2010) or to observe the perceptual and cognitive activities of trees (Trewavas 2003). Despite Meillassoux's insistence that "the human as a thinking being" is "*the insurpassable effect* of advent *ex nihilo*" (in Harman 2011b, 190), there are clear evolutionary links between the sentience of other organisms and our own. Indeed, even if we accept Meillassoux's overall argument for radical contingency, we should be suspicious of the way the particular contingencies, whose advent he narrates, all too conveniently place us at the center of everything, supposedly grounding "the legitimate superiority of humans over anonymous nature" (in Harman 2011b, 214).

For all these reasons, we need to be more attentive to, and critical of, the slippage by means of which Meillassoux moves from demanding that other entities in the cosmos be independent of *our* thinking about them to asserting that these other entities cannot possibly have any thought of their own. This also requires a broadening of perspective beyond

Meillassoux's unstated assumption that absolute a priori "intellectual intuition" is the only possible form of noncorrelational thought. I do not deny that *if* "intellectual intuition" exists at all (something of which I am not entirely convinced), then, on this planet, human beings seem to be the only entities capable of exercising it. But the point of referring to biological studies of affect, cognition, and decision in nonhuman organisms is to show that there are in fact many different kinds of thinking beyond both the purely rational and the intentional or correlational.

Recent biological research confirms Whitehead's overall sense that there are many forms of feeling, or of thought, "intermediate between the purely physical stage and the stage of conscious intellectual operations" (*PR*, 280). We need to maintain an open, pluralistic image of thought—or better, multiple images of thought—in order to avoid the mistake of rigidly dividing sapience from sentience and consigning everything that is not purely and abstractly rational into the category of deterministic causal mechanisms. Even just in human beings, there are many different degrees and forms of sentience and multifarious forms of perception, sensation, awareness, and cognition. Not all these modes of thought are rational, and not all of them are necessarily directed at objects. The range is even broader when we turn to consider other living things as well. Organisms like slime molds exhibit considerable cognitive accomplishments, although their "decision-making" process is "irrational" (Latty and Beekman 2010). And slime molds probably do not think according to our own all-too-human models of conscious intentionality. Even if human beings are inveterate correlationists, slime molds need not be.

Establishing just how slime molds actually think is, of course, a matter for empirical research. But whether we are concerned with the mentality of slime molds or with that of human beings, it is crucial not to limit our image of thought to rationalistic and/or intentionalistic models. In looking at how slime molds think, we may well discover not that they think like us but rather that we ourselves do not always think in the "human" ways we commonly suppose that we do. Far from "hypostasizing another form of our very humanity (sensation, will, perception, creation) across all of reality" (Meillassoux 2012, 4), as Meillassoux claims, such research seeks to discover modes of thought and action that are not predominantly "human" in the first place. There are several philosophical "lines of flight" away from the hegemonic (intentionalistic and correlational) image of thought. These approaches can help us understand how noncorrelational thought is possible and how it might work either in ourselves or in other entities.

One such "line of flight" is the *nonphilosophy* of François Laruelle. There are intriguing parallels between Laruelle's approach to standard philosophy and Meillassoux's critique of correlationism. Laruelle and Meillassoux both turn their attention to the ways in which reality exceeds—and escapes—our efforts to grasp it and define it. In order to do this, they both venture beyond the limits prescribed by the dominant forms of philosophy in order to approach a realm (Meillassoux's "great outdoors," Laruelle's One) that remains unthought. Whereas Meillassoux seeks to attain the reality of "an 'in itself' transcending all thought" (2012, 2), Laruelle seeks to affirm the Real "as non-determinable by thought and language ('foreclosed' to thought)" (1999, 138).

Moreover, both Meillassoux and Laruelle see the philosophical attempt to think reality in correlational terms as the consequence of an arbitrary *decision*. For Laruelle, every philosophy begins with a "philosophical Decision" that it cannot account for but that it nonetheless uses in order to ground its claims of comprehensiveness and self-sufficiency (Laruelle 1999, 143). "The philosophical Decision," Laruelle says, "is an operation of transcendence which believes (in a naïve and hallucinatory way) in the possibility of a unitary discourse on Reality" (2009, 56). In this way, the philosophical Decision is fundamentally correlational. It predetermines what can be thought, and it simply ignores, or rules out of existence, whatever it does not a priori include. The twin "fundamental decisions" of correlationism described by Meillassoux (2008, 49) exemplify this pattern quite well. The first correlationist decision "suffices to disqualify" any *reference* to what lies outside of the correlation (36); the second goes further by working to "*abolish* any . . . notion of the in-itself" altogether (37).

Given their common diagnosis of philosophy in its hegemonic correlational mode, Meillassoux and Laruelle also propose somewhat similar discursive strategies for extricating themselves from this matrix of thought. Both thinkers engage with, rather than simply dismissing, the philosophical positions from which they seek to escape. But "somewhat similar" does not mean "identical." Meillassoux and Laruelle differ most sharply in their particular *modes of engagement* with correlationism. Meillassoux insists that we cannot retreat to precorrelationist (i.e., pre-Kantian or pre-critical) dogmatism; "it is only by confronting the most radical form of the correlation" (Meillassoux 2008, 35) and pushing it to its utmost consequences that we can find the "faultline" (59) that allows us to overcome it. In this way, as Harman notes, Meillassoux "is actually *sympathetic* to the correlationalist position," for "he holds that correlationalism must be radicalized from within, not dismissed from the outside" as Harman himself would do (2009b, 164).

For his part, Laruelle does not demonstrate any such sympathy for traditional philosophy. He seeks not to overcome the philosophical Decision, nor to radicalize it from within, but rather to step back from it and suspend it. This means that Laruelle's nonphilosophy works, as John Mullarkey puts it, "by abstaining from philosophy as such while simultaneously taking it as its own raw material" (2006, 133). In this way, nonphilosophy necessarily acknowledges "the philosophical origin of the material from which its axioms and theorems are drawn"; it endeavors "to think by means of philosophy that which is no longer commensurate with the compass of philosophy, that which escapes its authority and its sufficiency" (Laruelle 1999, 143). Meillassoux and Laruelle alike seek to step away from the self-confirming totalizations of correlational thought. But whereas Meillassoux radicalizes and surpasses correlationism through an exacerbated form of dialectical speculation, Laruelle instead performs a radical withdrawal from speculation.

In consequence, there could not be a more radical contrast than that between Meillassoux's dualism and Laruelle's affirmation of radical immanence. Meillassoux, as we have seen, strives to evacuate intentionalistic thought entirely from the universe of things. But in counterpoint to a world without "givenness," he posits an entirely nonphenomenal "intellectual intuition of the absolute." Laruelle also seeks to attain what we might well call (following his own terminological practice) a *nonphenomenology*. But he does this precisely by rejecting both intellectual intuition and intentionality. Laruelle absolutely refuses anything like Meillassoux's division between things and thought. He insists instead on a "*nonintuitive phenomenality*," which manifests the "*radical immanence or immanence (to) itself*" of the Real, or of what he calls "the One" (Laruelle 1999, 141). This "non-intuitive phenomenality" cannot be a mode of thought *about* things, because it rather suggests that "all thought— including that of the 'highest' in philosophy—*is* a thing" already (Mullarkey 2012; emphasis added).

Nonphenomenological thought, Laruelle says, is "not a mode of perception . . . It is without intuitivity in general, neither an objective nor an intellectual intuition; and without thought or concept" (1999, 141). Elsewhere, he calls it "blind thought" (2011, 29) or "*irreflective* thought" (32). Noncorrelational thought is no more a "phenomenological phenomenon" (Laruelle 1999, 141) than it is an "intellectual intuition." Laruelle rejects the "natural perception" through which, for phenomenology, the "world is presented to the spectator" (Merleau-Ponty 2002, 216). Instead, he works through the way that photography, in its automaticity, performs a "radical critique" of perception (Laruelle 2011, 51), for photography offers us "a presentation that has never been affected and divided by a representation" (45). It "*lets things be*" without standing in for them or representing them (55); it produces a "semblance so extended that it is no longer an imitation, a tracing, an emanation, a 'representation' of what is photographed" but rather something entirely objective in itself (94). Photography thus exemplifies a mode of thought that *presents* things without being *about* them—that is, without representing them or *intending* them as objects.

A second, somewhat different, approach to noncorrelational thought is offered by Gilles Deleuze. In the first of his *Cinema* volumes, Deleuze writes of the "historical crisis of psychology" that arose at the end of the nineteenth century, at the very moment of the invention of the movies. This crisis concerned "the confrontation of materialism and idealism," leading to a "duality of image and movement, of consciousness and thing." At the time, Deleuze says, "two very different authors" made efforts to "overcome" the duality: Husserl and Bergson. "Each had his own war cry: all consciousness is consciousness *of* something (Husserl), or more strongly, all consciousness *is* something (Bergson)" (Deleuze 1986, 56).

Bergson's "war cry" resonates "more strongly" for Deleuze than Husserl's because Bergson's formulation short-circuits the correlation at the heart of phenomenology. It allows for sentience without reflexivity and for a kind of experience that remains "in-itself" without transcendence toward an external object. If "all consciousness *is* something," then thought immanently coincides with *matter* in "the absolute identity of the image and movement" (Deleuze 1986, 59). Therefore, as Deleuze puts it elsewhere, "it is not enough to say that consciousness is consciousness of something" (1994, 220); rather, we must move backward and downward in order to reach the primordial point at which "consciousness ceases to be a light cast upon objects in order to become a pure phosphorescence of things in themselves" (1990, 311). This also means that for Deleuze, the movies break with "natural perception" (Deleuze 1986, 57), just as the photograph does for Laruelle. Cinema "lacks a centre of anchorage and of horizon," Deleuze says (58), and for this reason, "the image exists in itself" (59), without reference or intentionality.

Noncorrelational thought happens on a level below or before what Deleuze calls the "structure-Other" (1990, 309ff.). Without the explicit presence of an Other to provide "a structure of the perceptual field" (307), such thought simply does not make the "distinction of consciousness and its object" (311). In this register, thinking—or better, sentience—is nonintentional and noncognitive. Quite literally, it is not involved in processes of cognition or re-cognition. It does not recognize or interpret anything; that is to say, it comes before—and it does not participate in—anything on the order of the Heideggerian "as-structure" or of what the cognitivist philosophers of mind describe as representationalist information processing.

We might well describe such noncorrelational thought or sentience as *autistic*—provided that we use this term in a nonpejorative and non-medicalized sense. As the neurodiversity movement helps us understand, autistic modes of thought should not be stigmatized as deficient just because they are evidently *different* from neurotypical ones (Savarese and Savarese 2010). Contrary to popular (and sometimes medical) prejudice, people along the autistic spectrum are not solipsists, and they are not lacking in empathy. Things may not be "given" or "manifested" to them in the ways that phenomenology describes; rather, they exhibit what Laruelle, in his book on photography, calls "an as-yet un-objectivating vision" (2011, 12). Their vision, like the "immanence-of-vision" (54) of the photograph for Laruelle, "makes everything it represents exist on a strictly 'equal footing'. Form and ground, recto and verso, past and future, foreground and distance, foreground and horizon, etc.—all this now exists fully outside any ontological hierarchy" (52). This flattening, Laruelle adds, leads not to a homogenization of experience but rather to "a liberation and an exacerbation of 'singularities' and 'materialities'" (52). Or, as Erin Manning puts it, in a different vocabulary, "the autistic dwells in an ecology of practices that creates resonances across scales and registers of life, both organic and inorganic" (2013, 225–26). Autistics are fully immersed in the world, immanently and without relations of phenomenological intentionality. In consequence, they seem to be less incorrigibly "correlationist" in their basic attunement to the world than neurotypicals are.

Noncorrelational sentience—conceived in these various ways by Laruelle, by Deleuze, and by theorists of autism—is an immanent attribute or power of being. It involves what Whitehead calls "feelings" (1929/1978, 40–42) rather than articulated judgments or Heideggerian implicit preunderstandings. It is nonintentional in that it is not directed toward, or correlated with, particular objects—though it may well be entwined or implicated with such objects. Noncorrelational sentience is "anoetic" (Tulving 1985, 3) and nonreflexive, and it may in many instances be nonconscious. It is a kind of phenomenality without phenomenology, or a nonconceptual "what-is-it-likeness." Noncorrelational sentience involves what Laruelle calls "a pure power of semblance" dissociated from any "representational content" (2011, 67). It experiences singularities that are, as Kant says of aesthetic sensations, "indeterminable and unfit for cognition" (2000, 216, 340), and it apprehends a "beauty" that, in the words of Metzinger, "is so subtle, so volatile as it were, that it evades cognitive access in principle" (2004, 73). In all these ways, noncorrelational sentience is *aesthetic*.

7 AISTHESIS

ALL VARIETIES OF SPECULATIVE REALISM, I have been arguing, must return to Kant in order to rework the terms of his settlement among conflicting philosophical claims. Only in this way is it possible for us to escape the correlational circle to which Kant would otherwise seem to have consigned us. Overall, Kant offers us a philosophy of finitude, which is to say one of limits that we can never get beyond. "Human reason" is confronted "with questions which it cannot dismiss . . . but which it also cannot answer, since they transcend every capacity of human reason" (Kant 1998, 99, Avii). We are irresistibly drawn to speculation, Kant says, but such speculation is always futile. For Kant, as Meillassoux puts it, "thought cannot get *outside itself*" (2008, 3) so as to access the "*great outdoors*, the *absolute* outside of pre-critical thinkers" (7). Any attempt to do so, Kant argues, will fail and only lead us instead into dogmatic illusion.

To restore the rights of what Whitehead calls "Speculative Philosophy" (*PR*, 3–17), we must somehow get around Kant's prohibition and find a way for thought to get "outside itself." Meillassoux, as we have seen, claims that the very structure of Kantian correlationism, if only it be pushed far enough, leads us beyond what, for Kant, was the limited "capacity of human reason"; once we recognize the contingency of the correlation, we are led to a more general understanding of the "absolute necessity of contingency" (Meillassoux 2008, 65) and therefore to an "intellectual intuition of the absolute" (82). Whereas Kant says that we cannot comprehend things in themselves, Meillassoux responds that this incomprehensibility is itself intrinsic to things in themselves rather than being due to our own intellectual limitations. The imperative for Meillassoux is therefore "*to put back into the thing itself what we mistakenly took to be an incapacity in thought*" (53). This reads to me like a "Bizarro World" inversion (or parody) of Hegel's dialectical critique of Kant. As Slavoj Žižek puts it, "the most elementary figure of dialectical reversal resides in transposing an epistemological obstacle into the thing itself" (2012, 17). But whereas Hegel puts our knowledge of things back into things themselves, Meillassoux puts our ignorance of things back into things themselves. Thus Hegel claims that we can, in fact, know Kantian noumena (things in themselves) because our own minds posited those things in the first place, whereas Meillassoux claims that we can know things in themselves precisely because we can be certain that our minds do not and cannot posit them and that they have "no reason" to be as they are (Meillassoux 2008, 60). In this way, Meillassoux founds a transcendent hyperrationalism on the irrationality of things in themselves.

But such inflated rationalism, present in opposite ways in Hegel and Meillassoux, is not the only route to circumventing Kant's prohibition. As Harman points out, Kant limits the possibilities of speculation not just because of the finitude of our own knowledge but also because he assumes the centrality of "the human–world relation" (2011b, 4). Meillassoux rejects finitude, but he ends up accepting anthropocentrism, for he not only affirms an absolute truth that human beings can know through speculation but also proclaims that "humans are in fact defined by their access to [this] truth" (in Harman 2011b, 190). Harman, in contrast, rejects anthropocentrism while affirming irreducible finitude. He "accepts the Kantian critique" that maintains "the impossibility of coincidence between a thing and the knowledge of that thing" (Harman 2011b, 133), but he argues that this not only applies to human beings; rather, we must extend "Kant's human–world duopoly" into a more "basic rift in the cosmos" that "lies between objects and relations in general" (Harman 2011c, 119). All modes of relation are necessarily finite and limited. No entity can ever grasp any other entity completely. The "knowledge of a house *is not itself a house*, and therefore any immanent model of philosophy is impossible" (Harman 2011b, 133).

This means that, for Harman no less than for Whitehead, "every actual entity, including God, is something individual for its own sake; and thereby transcends the rest of actuality" (*PR*, 88). Dogmatic certitude is therefore out of the question for Harman and Whitehead no less than for Kant. But Harman, like Whitehead, concludes from this not that speculation should be abandoned but rather that we can and must speculate. Philosophy, Harman says, should never follow the Kantian example and "convert objects into the conditions by which they can be known or verified" (2012a, 12). Rather, we should respect the *difference* of objects from their conditions of possibility. Precisely because our positive knowledge is limited, and because the world does not revolve around us, philosophy needs to speculate about all the things it cannot access directly. The knowledge we have is never sufficient, Harman says; at best, "we know without knowing, and think without thinking, by *alluding* to a thing rather than reducing it to a model contained within thought" (2011b, 152). For in the last analysis, "the real is something that cannot be known, only loved" (Harman 2012a, 12). In speculating about what it cannot know, philosophy expresses a "*love* of wisdom that makes no claim to be an actual wisdom" (15).

As I have already made clear, my own position puts me closer to Harman than to Meillassoux. With Harman, and against both Hegel and Meillassoux, I accept Kant's insistence on finitude. There is no such thing as absolute knowledge; even God, as Harman rightly says, cannot have it (2011b, 148). Yet I also diverge from Harman in one important respect: I think that Harman errs in conceiving finitude—just as Kant does in the first critique—as primarily a matter of the limits of *knowledge*. For Harman, every object is negatively characterized by its ultimate unknowability: its "withdrawal behind its accessibility to thought, a withdrawal that undercuts any immanent or absolute form of knowledge" (2011b, 149). I do not reject this formulation per se, but I think that it gives too much (negative) importance to questions of knowledge and certainty. As

Whitehead puts it, "the notion of mere knowledge is a high abstraction . . . conscious discrimination itself is a variable factor only present in the more elaborate examples of occasions of experience" (*AI*, 175–76). In fact, one object's *contact* with another—which is to say, an object's *being affected by* another—need not have anything to do with knowledge at all. Most interactions among entities take place, as Whitehead suggests, without involving any sort of "conscious knowledge" whatsoever (*PR*, 177). I am touched and moved by things without necessarily understanding them and even when they are not in themselves "accessible to [my] thought."

In Harman's own example of the finitude of knowledge, the moon "continues to orbit and sleep and attract in a way that our knowledge of the Moon cannot fathom and certainly cannot replace" (2011b, 148). But isn't this precisely the point? In orbiting the earth and gravitationally attracting the tides—not to mention emotionally attracting our fancies and contributing to the overall ambiance in which we live—the moon continually influences us, affects us, and has an impact on us, regardless of what we know—or do not know—about it. The moon touches us even in its "sleep"—that is, even when it is not concerned with us and not overtly directed toward us. In some cases—but not in all—we may well become cognizant, retroactively, of some of the ways in which the moon has *already* touched us and changed us. But its influence on us cannot be limited just to this. Finitude, therefore, means not only that there are limits to our knowledge of the moon but also—and much more importantly—that there are limits to our independence from the moon.

In other words, every object may well be "withdrawn" *epistemologically* from all the others, but this need not mean that objects are "barricaded behind firewalls" (Harman 2005, 188), separated from one another ontologically and aesthetically. If anything, epistemological withdrawal only exacerbates what Harman might well call the "sensual" implication or entwinement of objects with one another (Harman 2011a, 20–34). Harman himself is not blind to such connections. Whenever he turns to the effects that objects evidently *do* have on one another—despite his insistence that every object "is a dark crystal veiled in a private vacuum"

(47)—Harman rightly describes this mode of connection in aesthetic terms rather than cognitive or epistemological ones. For Harman, things affect other things indirectly, by means of what he calls *allure* or *vicarious causation*. An object that contacts us from outside, and whose true inner nature we cannot know, has a "basically ineffable effect on us" (Harman 2007b, 199). A "fusion" takes place, but one that "remains only partial, encrusted with residual accidents" (204). *Allure* means that one object calls to another from a vast distance; this is why "allure merely alludes to the object without making its inner life directly present" (199). In this indirect and "asymmetrical" way, Harman says, "two objects . . . touch without touching" (204).

Of course, this sort of indirect touch is not the "efficient causation" described by physical science (Harman 2007b, 174), and it has little to do with the commonsense image of direct cause and effect as what happens when one billiard ball smacks into another. Harman describes causation as a *vicarious* process because it involves a kind of substitution, or translation, or transfer at a distance. In short, causation is *occult influence*. Contact is never literal for Harman but rather a *metaphor*, which of course etymologically means a "transfer" or "carrying across" (2005, 101–24). Change is an aesthetic transformation; it happens when one object, or one quality of an object, stands in for and replaces another. In this way, aesthetics is the key to causality. Rather than explaining aesthetic influence as a diminished and distanced form of physical cause and effect, let alone as a symbolic representation of physical processes, Harman inverts the terms. He seeks to explain causality itself as an offshoot, or an extrapolation, of a more primordial process of aesthetic influence. Causation, Harman says, is "strangely akin to the allure of aesthetic experience" (2011a, 105). The object-oriented ontology (OOO) thinker Timothy Morton puts this point even more strongly, arguing in his book *Realist Magic* that action always takes place "at a distance" and therefore "causality is wholly an aesthetic phenomenon" (2013).

Harman's and Morton's views of causation are evidently at odds not only with the commonsense view that Morton dismissively calls "clunk causality" (2013) but also with most recent philosophical discussions of cause and effect. Modern philosophy, from Descartes onward, defines itself in opposition to the Aristotelian and Scholastic analyses of causation. Aristotle's fourfold classification of causes is rejected, together with the very idea of causation as an intrinsic process. Hume and Kant both locate causal relations not in things themselves but only in the mind that contemplates them. According to Hume, we can never experience (or even perceive) causality itself; we only infer its existence from our observations of "constant conjunctions" of events. In the contemporary version of this account, maintained by the late analytic philosopher David Lewis, "necessary connections" among separate entities do not and cannot exist, since "all there is to the world is a vast mosaic of local matters of particular fact, just one little thing and then another" (1986, ix). Causal connections therefore lack all necessity, as they are nothing more than repeated events, or regularities, which we have historically observed to "supervene" on these "local matters of fact." There are many "possible worlds" in which things act differently than they do in this one, and these possible worlds are themselves, in their own manner, entirely real. Causality in *our* world can only be defined counterfactually: when I say that A caused B, all this means is that if A had not happened, then B would not have happened either. I can give no deeper (or more intrinsic) reason for *why* this should be the case.

As for Kant, he is worried about the skeptical consequences that can follow from Hume's argument. If no deeper reason can be given for why A causes B—or, more precisely, for why B always seems to follow A—then we have no assurance that nature is lawful and regular and that this "constant conjunction" will still take place in the future. Nothing in Hume's account guarantees the reliability of induction. But despite his unease, Kant never disputes Hume's fundamental premises. He accepts Hume's denial of necessary connections among entities in the world, as well as Hume's assumption that it is only in the observing mind that such connections are ever made. Therefore, in order to restore certainty and give a firm foundation to physical science, Kant assigns necessity to what for Hume was only an empirically established habit. That is to say, whereas Hume notes that our minds infer relations of cause and effect, Kant establishes the inference of causality as a Category of the Understanding: something that is imposed by our own minds on the world that we perceive. Causality may not exist among things in themselves, Kant says, but it is an indispensable part of our subjective experience. Or, as Meillassoux paraphrases Kant's argument, "causal necessity" is not "absolutely necessary" in and of itself, but it "is a necessary condition for the existence of consciousness and the world it experiences" (2008, 89). Without causal necessity, things would fall apart; neither the subject-self nor the object-world would be able to subsist. This is, of course, the founding premise of correlationism.

Since Meillassoux seeks to undo correlationism from within, he repeats Kant's analysis in reverse. He rejects the solution provided by Kant's "Analytic of Concepts" and reverts to "Hume's Problem" about causality (Meillassoux 2008, 82–111). Hume wonders how to ground causal necessity, since we always assume it but cannot find it presented to us directly in experience. Whereas Kant replies by providing a ground for causal necessity in the workings of the mind, Meillassoux argues that, for rational thought, "the obvious falsity of causal necessity is blindingly evident" (91). The audacity of this claim is dazzling. Hume worries about the fact that although we observe constant conjunctions, we never observe a power that enforces these conjunctions. He is disturbed that we cannot help but assume causality, even though there is no sensory evidence to back it up. But Meillassoux entirely inverts this logic; he goes so far as to claim that "it is our senses that impose this belief in causality upon us, not thought" (91). In warning us to distrust the evidence of the senses and to follow the guidance of pure reason alone, Meillassoux makes a Platonic argument rather than a Humean or empiricist one. By doing this, he transforms Hume's epistemological doubt about causality into a positive ontological doctrine. There is no way to discover causal necessity among things in themselves, because such relations simply do not and cannot exist. It is a priori necessary that causal relations be merely contingent. Hyperbolizing a statement of Hume's, Meillassoux maintains that, in point of fact, "the same cause may actually bring about 'a hundred different events' (and even many more)" (90). One cannot even reason about causes and effects probabilistically, as Humeans like Lewis endeavor to do. Whereas Lewis considers degrees of justified belief and the counterfactual cases of various "possible worlds," Meillassoux rejects the very idea that "the possible" can be "totalized," or subject to any sort of statistical distribution (Meillassoux 2008, 105–6).

All these theories of causality—Hume's, Kant's, and Meillassoux's—are antirealist ones: they all start from the unquestioned assumption that causality cannot actually result from the actual properties of things in themselves. In a world with no "necessary connections," it is only the human mind that extrapolates from particular events in order to posit causal relations between one thing and another. Harman might well accept the first half of this argument, since he opposes all forms of what he calls "relationism" (2009b, 75) and maintains that "real objects" are entirely isolated from one another and cannot ever affect one another; therefore, there can be no necessary connections. However, Harman also holds that every object has deep essential properties, including "inherent causal power" (2011a, 21), and this is something that Hume, Kant, Lewis, and Meillassoux all deny.

More generally, Harman argues that the greatest "litmus test" for any philosophy is to "ask . . . whether it places inanimate relations on the same footing as the relations between human and world" (2009b, 67). A truly realist philosophy must be able to speak of the ways that objects interact with, or affect, one another in the absence of a human (or animal) observer—rather than privileging the special relation between objects and an observing (animal, human, or rational) subject. The interaction between cotton and fire must be granted the same ontological status as the interaction of a human mind with either (Harman 2005, 170). From this point of view, theories that restrict causality to being a projection or imposition by the human mind are obviously deficient. A nonanthropocentric, realist analysis of causality is needed: one that is not just restricted to the question of how causal relations appear *to us*.

Such a realist account of cause and effect is proposed by George Molnar (2007) and more fully elaborated by Stephen Mumford and Rani Lill Anjum (2011). These analytic philosophers are realists, in the first instance, about the *powers* possessed by various entities. Molnar argues that "powers are intrinsic properties of their bearers"—this stands in opposition to the more common assumption (maintained by Hume and Lewis, among others) that "a power is really nothing over and above the possibility of manifestation" (2007, 57). That is to say, the causal powers possessed by things are entirely ontologically real. Salt is soluble; my drinking glass is fragile; this knife is sharp. Such qualities or capacities may only be manifested under particular circumstances; nonetheless, these "inherent causal powers" are real, intrinsic properties of the objects that bear them, and this is the case even if the salt never encounters water and never dissolves, even if the glass never breaks, and even if the knife never actually cuts anything. If solubility, fragility, and sharpness are intrinsic properties of things, then we cannot explain them away, as Lewis seeks to do, by invoking hypothetical counterfactuals.

Molnar's line of thought here is not far from Spinoza's (pre-Kantian) notion that things have the intrinsic ability to affect or to be affected by other things. An object's powers are *directed toward* other objects, for it is only in encounters with other objects that these powers are enacted. Yet at the same time, this does not mean that powers are defined relationally or that they are anything less than intrinsic to their bearers. As Molnar strikingly writes, "while ontologically there is nothing over and above individuals and their properties (actions), *causally* there is" (2007, 198). This separation of the *causal* from the *ontological* is crucial. On the ontological level, Molnar agrees with Hume and Lewis that there is nothing besides local matters of fact. Harman might well object that this implies an "undermining" of objects by reducing them to their subatomic constituents (2011a, 8–10); nonetheless, such a position is at least not incompatible with Harman's claim that objects have a substantial reality outside of, and anterior to, their relations. Molnar would also not disagree with Harman's argument that an object's properties are always fully actual and intrinsic (rather than potential or virtual), even when they are not currently being enacted (Harman 2009b, 130). For Molnar, however, this intrinsic reality is itself largely composed of actual *causal abilities* to *do things*: to perform directed actions and thereby to interact relationally with other things. Because the properties of individual things are powers, they make possible a substantial sort of causality "over and above" local matters of fact. This is something that Lewis does not recognize and that Harman consigns to the secondary, "sensual" realm. But for Molnar, when things contingently encounter other things, real effects (and not merely "sensual" ones) are produced.

Following from Molnar's realism about powers, Mumford and Anjum argue for a realist approach to causality: "Effects are brought about by powers manifesting themselves" (2011, 7). The properties of things just are "clusters of causal powers," and when something happens, these properties "are doing the causal work" (3). Causality thus exists objectively in the world; it is not just something inferred (or imposed) by an observer. Both in ourselves and in all other entities, causal powers are entirely real. This is still the case even when these powers do not have the opportunity to manifest themselves or when their manifestation is thwarted by countervailing powers (as when I try to light a match, but wind blows out the flame). But even in cases of successful manifestation, powers do not express themselves totally. Here Mumford and Anjum are close to Manuel Delanda, who similarly argues that a thing's capacities "form a potentially open list, since there is no way to tell in advance in what way a given entity may affect or be affected by innumerable other entities" (2006, 10). There is always more to a thing's powers than the particular *effects* that these powers help produce in one or another instance.

If we accept this realist account of causality, then Harman is entirely right to contend that every "event can be seen to hold something in reserve behind its current sum total of effects" (2005, 232). Since powers are actual attributes of objects, they are fully real, even when they are not being manifested. Moreover, these powers are not exhausted by, and cannot be reduced to, their particular manifestations. Objects are always more than what they do, and for this reason, when we see them in action, "we can only *allude* to their innermost reality" (Harman 2005, 107). For Mumford and Anjum, just as for Harman, the entities that affect one another nonetheless "fail to exhaust each other's depths" (Harman 2005, 55). The moon is not only more than what I know of it; it is also more than what it does to me, and indeed more than the sum of its effects on all other entities.

My own agreement and disagreement with Harman—my revision, or "translation," of his thought—can now be stated as follows: I accept Harman's account of causality as aesthetic interaction, but I reject the deep background of ontologically distinct substances within which he places this account. It is evident that a thing may affect me without my having access to the "inner life" of the thing, or it to mine. This follows both from the realist account of causality proposed by Molnar, Mumford, and Anjum and from Harman's suggestion that causal contact is superficial and non-totalizing. But I cannot see why it should follow from all this that "the object in its inner life is never touched by any of the entities that bump, crush, meddle, or carouse with it" (Harman 2005, 73). For even if you know nothing of my inner life, your actions may well affect it profoundly. I am always being affected and altered by things that call to me, or brush up against me, or delight or repulse me, or otherwise superficially encounter me. Indeed, these things affect my inner life *precisely because* they remain separate from me. I cannot simply incorporate them within myself. Even the food I eat doesn't just become more of myself. It has a distinct aesthetic effect on me through its aroma and taste, as well as through the physical and psychological changes that it induces within my body.

Another way to put this is to say that, contrary to what the systems theorists tell us, neither my own "self" nor any other entity is "operationally closed." The OOO thinker Levi Bryant, adopting the notion of *operational closure* from Maturana and Varela and from Niklas Luhmann, defines it to mean, first, that "the operations of an autopoietic system refer only to themselves and are products of the system itself," and, second, that "autopoietic systems are closed in on themselves, that they do not relate directly to an environment, that they do not receive information from an environment" (Bryant 2011, 149). But aesthetic causality, as I have been describing it, violates both of these conditions, for my aesthetic contact with another object always occurs over an unbridgeable distance. This means, first, that it involves a reference—an *allusion*, in Harman's terminology—to something beyond and outside of myself, and, second, that this allusive, external reference is irreducible to myself and resists assimilation into the terms that define "myself" as a coherent system. In consequence, my own actions or "operations" *never* "refer only to themselves"; they always relate directly to things and forces that are outside their power and beyond their reach.

Bryant seeks to explain away what I am calling "aesthetic contact" as a "perturbation or irritation" to the system whose "information value . . . is constituted strictly by the distinctions belonging to the organization of the autopoietic machine itself" (Bryant 2011, 149–50). But this wrongly assumes that encounters between entities can be fully described in terms of "information" (which is to say, in terms of Spencer Brown's and Luhmann's "distinctions" or Gregory Bateson's "difference which makes a difference"). To the contrary, transfers and dissipations of energy, provoked by forces external to a "system," can never adequately be encoded in such informational terms. There is always a remainder that the system in question cannot refer back to itself, and this failure points to a dimension of contact that is not reducible to cognition or recognition. Once the "perturbation" passes a certain threshold, it can no longer be expressed in terms of, or assimilated to, the system's own preestablished "distinctions." Luhmann's and Bryant's theory of autopoiesis once again wrongly poses the question of limits and finitude, and therefore of aesthetic relations, only in epistemological terms.

We should not be troubled by Harman's discovery that causal effects are partial and indirect, which is to say *aesthetic*, for this *just is* the way that causality actually *works*. As Mumford and Anjum put it, "the connection between a causal set up and its effect is . . . an irreducibly dispositional one"; it is "not reducible to pure necessity or pure contingency," but "something in between" (2011, 175). That is to say, causal relations are never complete and never entirely deterministic; they are *always* partial and indirect. "The modality of dispositionality," Mumford and Anjum tell us, "cannot be captured in other, non-dispositional, terms" (176). Kant is wrong when he seeks to establish the necessity of causal relations, but Hume, Lewis, and Meillassoux are equally wrong when they interpret the lack of necessity as implying sheer contingency, or mere "supervenience."

It does not follow from all this that "real" objects are therefore inviolate. There is nothing unreal about bumping, crushing, meddling, or carousing. Such modes of affecting and being affected only seem deficient in contrast to some supposed mode of total fusion that (as Harman himself shows) is impossible anyway. What Harman dismisses as the merely "sensual" realm of carnality, causality, and aesthetics is in fact the only realm there is: it is the actual place and time in which events happen and within which things both "withdraw" from one another and show themselves to one another. "If we ask where this vicarious causation occurs," Harman writes, "the answer is that it lies on the interior of a further entity, in the molten core of an object" (2005, 232). But there is no spatiotemporal location that is not such a "molten core."

This point can be put in still another way. For Harman, perception and thought are *exclusively* relational activities, which never touch the inner essences of things. Thought is always intentional, in the phenomenological sense: it is always directed at something, always *about* something. But this means that there is no room for thought on the most fundamental level of being, where objects are "withdrawn absolutely from all relation" (Harman 2005, 76). In their innermost essence, Harman says, not only are objects inaccessible to any sort of mental or physical contact; they also do not perceive or think on their own account. Harman concedes that "anything that *relates* must perceive," and thereby think, but because relations are inessential, "this means that entities have psyches accidentally, not in their own right" (2008, 9).

Harman therefore claims that an entity can subsist without relating to anything else at all and thus without thinking. He tells us, in some quite lovely prose, that "the name for an object that exists without relating, exists without perceiving, is a *sleeping* entity, or a *dormant* one . . . Dormant objects are those which are real, but currently without psyche. Each night we make ourselves as dormant as we can, stripping away the accidental accretions of the day and gathering ourselves once more in the essential life where we are untouched by external relations" and therefore unmoved by thought (2008, 9). Harman imagines a scenario in which objects lie inert, like Tennyson's Kraken—or Lovecraft's Cthulhu, for that matter—in an "ancient, dreamless, uninvaded sleep."

But can this really be true? Is sleep ever truly "dreamless" and "uninvaded"? When I hear this claim, I cannot forbear from asking, "To sleep, perchance to dream"? To the extent that dreaming is private, nonrelational, and purely internally generated, its very possibility nonetheless shows us that the psyche still exists and functions even in the absence of external perception, stimulation, or other form of contact. Thinking still happens nonrelationally and without having any sort of "intentional object." On the other hand, to the extent that dreaming *does* respond—however indirectly—to events outside the dreamer, we have evidence that "withdrawal" is never total or absolute. Of course, dreamers need not be—and usually are not—explicitly aware of the external events that stimulate their dreams and to which their dreaming is an oblique response. Things continue to affect the dreamer, even though the dreamer does not have any *knowledge* of such things. Harman seems to envisage ontological withdrawal as an impossibly dreamless sleep, one altogether devoid of thought or sensation and therefore blissfully free from any sort of relation whatsoever. But such a state is never achieved short of death or (in the case of inanimate entities) physical dissolution. A thing only becomes absolutely insentient, or nonrelational, at the point where it disaggregates and ceases to exist.

Where Harman speaks of "touch without touching," therefore, I would rather designate this causal and affective process positively as *contact at a distance*. Think of it as a sort of sensibility, or sensitivity, without knowledge and without phenomenological intentionality: it is not that touching over a distance doesn't "really" happen, as Harman seems to imply, but rather that the touch itself occurs, first of all, in a mode that is not accessible to cognition or to knowledge. It may be that, as in a dream, I do not perceive what touches me at all but only feel its effects allusively and metaphorically, in an entirely different register. Or it may be that the touch only reaches me implicitly and tentatively, like a mere grazing of the skin or a subtle infiltration. Or else it may be that an erotic or mortal touch overwhelms me so utterly that I am unable to process it cognitively. In all these cases, aesthetic contact happens in the first instance outside knowledge, on a level beneath the threshold of conscious perception or beyond its capacities to recognize or relate. Outside of any correlation of "subject" and "object," or "knower" and "known," an occult process of influence is already taking place. Harman is entirely right to say that this sort of touching involves "a secret content that is never presentable" (2005, 124). But even though aesthetic contact is *vicarious*, or *aesthetic*, it does indeed involve the real manifestation of real powers, with real consequences, and sometimes even calamitous ones.

My own version of speculative realism therefore focuses not on epistemological questions at all but rather directly on aesthetics, for aesthetics is the realm of immanent, noncognitive contact. It must be situated before—or better, on the hither side—of knowledge. Indeed, we can find hints of this already in Kant's own discussion of aesthetics in the first half of the *Critique of Judgment*. In the "Analytic of the Beautiful," in particular, Kant opens up a path not taken elsewhere and allows us to glimpse speculative possibilities that are otherwise excluded by the architectonics of his system. It remains the case that Kant never lets us step *outside* of the correlational circle. But Kant's aesthetics occupies a moment that *precedes* the very construction of this circle: precedes it both logically and temporally. For Kant, there can be no *au delà*, no movement beyond phenomena to an "intellectual intuition" of things in themselves. But Kantian aesthetics nonetheless offers us an *en deçà*: a movement that *comes before*, or that *falls short of*, the correlation of mind and being and of subject and object. In this way,

Kantian aesthetics sidesteps the straightjacket of correlationism while still being grounded in finitude.

Kantian aesthetics is premised on a strange resonance—or what might better be called a kind of short circuit—between singularity and universality. These two extremes come into an immediate, noncognitive contact, bypassing all hierarchies, all mediations, and all intermediate levels of organization. How is this possible? For Kant, the Beautiful is not an objective category. The aesthetic "does not contain an objective quantity of judgment, but only a subjective one" (Kant 2000, 100, 214). Beauty is not a Platonic Form whose existence would somehow precede our own and to whose outlines actual beautiful things would have to conform. Beauty is also not a genus of which particular beautiful things would be the species. Any such hierarchical classification is impossible, because "all judgments of taste"—and therefore of beauty—"are *singular* judgments" (100, 215). This means that every instance of beauty is something new, without grounding, justification, or precedent. A beautiful work of art is a production for which "no determinate rule can be given" in advance (186, 307). In this way, every instance of beauty is unlike every other. Beautiful objects are never fully commensurable with other objects, nor even with one another.

However, although judgments of beauty are singular and their "determining ground *cannot* be *other than subjective*" (Kant 2000, 89, 203), this does not mean that they are *merely* subjective. The beautiful must be distinguished from the simply "agreeable," no less than from the "good" (Kant 2000, 97–98, 212–13). The beautiful is not anything like what we would characterize today—in a world organized around the assumptions of cognitive psychology and "rational choice" theory—as an individual (or consumer) "preference." Beauty is not a matter of personal "interest" (90–91, 204–5); it cannot be attributed to the whims or cravings of an isolated subject. "It would be ridiculous," Kant says, for anyone to speak of something as being "beautiful *for me*" (98, 212), for a judgment of beauty, in contrast to a mere personal preference, necessarily "*demands* . . . the assent of everyone" (98, 213).

The only thing that singular aesthetic judgments have in common is that they *all* make such an absolute demand. Each of them affirms itself to infinity without compromise or limit. Each of them proclaims itself in the same way: with "a *universal voice*" (Kant 2000, 101, 216). A judgment of beauty, Kant says, is "a representation which, though singular and without comparison to others, nevertheless is in agreement with the *conditions* of universality" (104, 219; emphasis added). But how are such conditions expressed, and how can they be obtained? In considering such questions, Kant prefigures Deleuze's doctrine of the *univocity* of being. What Kant presents as an exceptional situation—since it applies to judgments of beauty, but not to our general knowledge of objects—becomes a basic ontological principle for Deleuze. *Univocity* means, for Deleuze, "not that Being is said in a single and same sense, but that it is said, in a single and same sense, *of* all its individuating differences or intrinsic modalities" (1994, 36). In other words, the being of any one thing is different from the being of any other thing, but being per se is identically *attributed* to all things. All modalities of being are singularities, but all these singularities inhere in Being *in the same way*, and for this reason, they all affirm themselves in the same way. There is a parallel, not of essence, but of *manner*. And that is how singularity resonates with universality, without the need for any sort of mediation.

If each instance of beauty is singular and not subject to mediation, this means that—even in its universal reach—it does not fit under any concept or category. Beauty "contributes nothing to cognition" (Kant 2000, 90, 204) but rather always precedes it. We *sense* or *feel* that something is beautiful even before we recognize it and without necessarily knowing anything about it. "The judgment of taste is not a cognitive judgment," Kant says, "and hence it is neither *grounded* on concepts nor *aimed* at them" (95, 209). Rather, a sense of beauty arises directly, "without the mediation of concepts" (101, 216). I have an immediate "feeling of pleasure or displeasure" when I encounter the object (89, 203). In this way, Kantian aesthetic judgment is quite close to what Whitehead calls *feeling*, or primordial "appetites in the form of aversions and adversions" (*PR*, 32). For

Whitehead, we always take up incoming "data" in ways that are "emotional, purposive, appreciative" (*PR*, 85). Every occasion of experience has a "subjective form" that expresses "qualities of joy and distaste, of adversion and of aversion" (*PR*, 234).

The most vexing issue in Kant's aesthetics is his notorious claim that aesthetic judgment is *disinterested* (Kant 2000, 91, 205). How does this square with the notion that aesthetic judgment has to do with pleasure and displeasure? How is a disinterested pleasure even possible? Kant's notion of aesthetic disinterest has frequently been mocked and rejected as self-evidently ridiculous—most famously, perhaps, by Nietzsche, who invokes beauty "as a great *personal* fact and experience, as a fund of strong personal experiences, desires, surprises and pleasures" (Nietzsche 1997, 116). But Nietzsche's sneering criticism is based on a misunderstanding. The idea of disinterest follows closely from Kant's insistence that beauty is nonconceptual and that nothing is beautiful just *for me*. "Disinterested" does not mean "dispassionate" or "devoid of feeling"; indeed, these latter terms better apply to objective cognition. Rather, in Kant's use of the term, *disinterested* means something more like "vicarious," or "by substitution." Aesthetic pleasure can best be described as *vicarious sensation* or *vicarious enjoyment*. We are not far from Harman's idea of *vicarious causation*. In aesthetic feeling, something that is not mine, and that I cannot assimilate into myself, is nevertheless directly communicated to me. I do not get to know the thing, but I *allude* to it, transforming it over a distance.

In other words, even though beauty is a matter of sensuous immediacy and even though its basis "*cannot* be *other than subjective*," nonetheless it cannot be tied down to the particular situation in which I apprehend it. My finding something beautiful depends neither on my own subjective needs and desires nor on the actual circumstances of my encounter with the beautiful object. The singular instance of beauty that I apprehend is independent of all these particularities; it is *citational* or *iterable*, as Derrida might say, and therefore transportable elsewhere. This is because it is not really I myself, as a concrete individual, who makes a subjective judgment of beauty. Rather, the point of an aesthetic judgment—its claim to speak, despite being subjective, in a *universal voice*—is that the "I" who makes it is no one in particular, but could be *anyone*. Aesthetic judgment speaks to what Giorgio Agamben calls "whatever being": that which is "neither particular nor general, neither individual nor generic" (1993, 1 and 107). At least in principle, an instance of beauty ought to be able to appeal to anyone else in the same way that it appeals to me.

Aesthetic disinterest also means that the question of actual existence—of whether the object that pleases me is real or fictional—is suspended. Kant says that a judgment of beauty is "indifferent with regard to the existence of an object" (2000, 95, 209). How can this be? Kant famously argues in the first critique that "*Being* is obviously not a real predicate" (1998, 567, A598/B626), thus refuting the "ontological proof" of the existence of God. We cannot, Kant says, list "necessary existence" as one of God's attributes and on that basis claim that he must exist, for "not the least bit gets added to the thing when I posit in addition that this thing *is*" (567, A599/B627). In the third critique, Kant implicitly relies on a similar logic. Every judgment of beauty feels, and responds to, "the *form of the purposiveness* of an object" (Kant 2000, 106, 221). But because existence is not a predicate, the matter of the object's existence or nonexistence does not enter into this "form" at all, and therefore it cannot enter into my aesthetic response to the object. Aesthetic feeling remains vicarious, no matter how intense it is.

Indeed, if I were to take the actual existence (or not) of the object into consideration, then I would be making either a cognitive or a moral judgment rather than an aesthetic one. For Kant, a cognitive judgment is objective; its empirical truth is entirely independent of the person making it. A moral judgment is categorical or universally binding; it commands obedience absolutely, without exception. Both cognitive and moral judgments apply unreservedly to everyone. This is very different from the way an aesthetic judgment, with merely "subjectively universal validity" (Kant 2000, 100, 215), only appeals ungroundedly to *anyone*. (Kant himself does not actually employ the verbal distinction between *everyone* and *anyone*, but it is a useful way to explain and designate the difference in principle on which he does insist.) The universality of a cognitive or a moral judgment is intrinsically given right from the beginning. But aesthetic judgment—which is to say, the affirmation of an ungrounded singularity— "does not itself *postulate* the accord of everyone . . . it only *ascribes* this agreement to everyone" (101, 216). Therefore an aesthetic judgment— unlike a cognitive or a moral one—cannot command assent but only request it or demand it. Such a judgment "expects confirmation . . . only from the consent of others" (101, 216): a consent that must be freely given. The "universality" of an aesthetic judgment is therefore not established in advance but needs to be *produced* through an ongoing process of solicitation and communication.

In all these ways, Kantian aesthetic judgment, like Whiteheadian "feeling," is a *response* to an object that is encountered in the course of experience. But because it is not cognitive and not objective, such judgment or feeling is not really *about* the object to which it responds. Through aesthetic judgment, Kant says, "nothing at all in the object is designated" (2000, 89, 203). And every "adversion" or "aversion," Whitehead says, is an unforced "decision" on the part of an actual entity in response to the data that it encounters (*PR*, 254). In either case, what we get is not a (more or less accurate) internal representation of the object but rather an ungrounded aesthetic "valuation" of the object—an evaluation either "upward" or "downward" (*PR*, 254). Even though aesthetic feeling is *triggered* by an object, the feeling itself is independent of any intentional relation to the object. Aesthetic feelings with regard to an object cannot be *correlated* to that object. An aesthetic encounter takes place without recognition or possession and without phenomenological intentionality or "aboutness."

Kantian aesthetic judgment thus involves a kind of sentience that is more than just the passive reception of sensible intuition but less than conscious recognition and comprehension. The "Analytic of Concepts" in the first critique operates according to what Gilbert Simondon calls a *hylemorphic schema* (2005, 39–51): a dualism according to which an active form is imposed on a passive, and initially formless, matter or content. The "categories of the understanding" are the basic principles according to which all experience must be organized, and what Kant calls *schemata* work to guide the ways in which these categories are applied in practice. For Kant, this is the only way that perception can be more than chaotic and that positive knowledge can be organized. But in the third critique—in contrast to the first—all this creaky machinery breaks down. Everything important happens immanently, *in between* the dualist poles of activity and passivity, subject and object, or form and content. Indeed, from the point of view of aesthetic judgment, we can retrospectively regard Kant's formulations of passive intuition on the one hand and active understanding on the other as abstractions from the initially vague and intermediate process of what Whitehead calls "sense-reception" (as opposed to "sense-perception"; *PR*, 113).

Kant defines *beauty* as "an *intuition* (of the imagination) for which a concept can never be found adequate" (2000, 218, 342). In other words, beauty involves an immediate excess of sensation: something that stimulates thinking but that cannot be contained in, or expressed by, any particular thought. There is an overflow of perceptual experience that cannot be categorized or contained, much less put into language. An "aesthetic idea" is one "that occasions much thinking without it being possible for any determinate thought, i.e. *concept*, to be adequate to it, which, consequently, no language fully attains or can make intelligible" (192, 314). Beauty impels us to think, but it cannot itself be thought.

As happens so often in the third critique, Kant's formulation here prefigures both Whitehead and Deleuze. Inciting thought while also escaping thought, the Kantian "aesthetic idea" is what Whitehead calls a "lure for feeling" (*PR*, 85 and passim). In the contemplation of beauty, "imaginative feeling" is more important than "intellectual belief" (*PR*, 187); "judgment is eclipsed by aesthetic delight" (*PR*, 185). In Deleuze's similar formulation, "something in the world forces us to think. This something is an object not of recognition but of a fundamental *encounter*" (1994, 139). The object provokes thought without letting itself be thought; we are *forced to think* precisely because we have come across something that our thought cannot capture or identify, much less recognize. Deleuze's object of encounter is therefore not an "intentional object" in the phenomenological sense; rather, it is something that is not a correlate of my thought, something that thought cannot possibly correlate to itself.

In all these ways, aesthetics marks the place where cognition and correlationism get left behind—or better, where they have not yet arisen. Although Kant explicitly seems to regard aesthetic judgment as just an exception from the otherwise necessary work of the understanding, his formulations implicitly suggest more than this. Deleuze notes that "the post-Kantians," seeking to improve on or complete Kant, "demanded a principle which was not merely conditioning in relation to objects but which was also truly genetic and productive" (1983, 51–52). But in the "Analytic of the Beautiful," as well as in the "Transcendental Aesthetic" that opens the first critique, Kant already offers us the rudiments of such an account of the genesis of thought. In Kant's implied narrative, affect precedes, and both exceeds and gives birth to, understanding. The "Transcendental Aesthetic" posits a primordial aesthetic sensibility in the form of our immersion in space and time. Although Kant credits the perceiving mind, rather than things in themselves, with articulating space and time, he nonetheless explains that space and time are not due to the understanding but precede it absolutely as "pure forms of all sensible intuition" (Kant 1998, 183, A39/B56). This means that space and time are neither "empirical concepts" nor "discursive concepts" (174–79, A23/B38–A32/B48). Indeed, although "time and space are . . . *sources* of cognition" (183, A38/B55; emphasis added), they are not in themselves cognitive or conceptual at all. The mind imposes the "Categories of the Understanding" on what Kant claims is otherwise an indeterminate flux of sensations, but space and time are already immanent to that flux. They precede, and are already presupposed by, any act of cognition whatsoever. This is what allows Deleuze to claim that a Bergsonian or Proustian apprehension of time is already at work in Kant: "Time is not internal to us, but . . . we are internal to time" (Deleuze 1989, 82).

In Kant's famous formula, "thoughts without content are empty; intuitions without concepts are blind" (1998, 193; B75/A51). But aesthetics modifies or suspends this principle. "Thoughts without content" remain "empty" in any case, but in the third critique, "intuitions without concepts" are no longer unthinkable. Aesthetic judgments are indeed "blind," because they are made without understanding and even without knowledge as to the actual existence of the object being apprehended. But this does not reduce them to nullity. Aesthetic feeling is immanent and uncategorizable *first of all*, but cognition could not happen without it. The primordial form of all experience, and thereby of all action and relation, is an aesthetic one. This is why Harman is right to proclaim that aesthetics is not "a local phenomenon of human experience," but rather "the root of all relations . . . including causal relations." Aesthetics "belongs to ontology as a whole, not to the special metaphysics of animal perception" (Harman 2007b, 205).

I very much doubt that the world can be "justified" as an "aesthetic phenomenon," as Nietzsche so stridently claimed (1999, 72). But justified or not, the world is indeed, at its base, aesthetic. And through aesthetics, we can act in the world and relate to other things in the world without reducing it and them to mere correlates of our own thought. This is why I propose a speculative aesthetics as an alternative both to Meillassoux's vision of radical contingency and to Harman's vision of objects encased in immutable vacuums. Such a speculative aesthetics is still to be constructed; Kant, Whitehead, and Deleuze only provide us with its rudiments. Indeed, since every aesthetic encounter is singular, anything like a *general aesthetics* is impossible. And so, rather than offer a stirring conclusion, I had better leave it at that.

BIBLIOGRAPHY

Agamben, Giorgio. 1993. *The Coming Community*. Translated by Michael Hardt. Minneapolis: University of Minnesota Press.

Badiou, Alain. 2000. *Deleuze: The Clamor of Being*. Translated by Louise Burchill. Minneapolis: University of Minnesota Press.

Barad, Karen. 2007. *Meeting the Universe Halfway: Quantum Physics and the Entanglement of Matter and Meaning*. Durham, N.C.: Duke University Press.

Benjamin, Walter. 2003. *Selected Writings, Volume 4: 1938–1940*. Edited by Howard Eiland and Michael W. Jennings. Translated by Edmund Jephcott et al. Cambridge, Mass.: Belknap Press of Harvard University Press.

Bennett, Jane. 2010. *Vibrant Matter: A Political Ecology of Things*. Durham, N.C.: Duke University Press.

Bhaskar, Roy. 1975. *A Realist Theory of Science*. New York: Routledge, reprinted 2008.

Blamauer, Michael, ed. 2012. *The Mental as Fundamental: New Perspectives on Panpsychism*. Frankfurt: Ontos Verlag.

Bogost, Ian. 2012. *Alien Phenomenology, or What It's Like to Be a Thing*. Minneapolis: University of Minnesota Press.

Brandom, Robert. 2009. *Reason in Philosophy: Animating Ideas*. Cambridge, Mass.: Harvard University Press.

Brassier, Ray. 2007. *Nihil Unbound: Enlightenment and Extinction*. New York: Palgrave Macmillan.

———. 2011. "I Am a Nihilist Because I Still Believe in Truth." http://www.kronos.org.pl/index.php?23151,896.

Brassier, Ray, Iain Hamilton Grant, Graham Harman, and Quentin Meillassoux. 2007. "Speculative Realism." *Collapse: Philosophical Research and Development* 3:307–449.

Braver, Lee. 2007. *A Thing of This World: A History of Continental Anti-Realism*. Evanston, Ill.: Northwestern University Press.

Brembs, Bjorn. 2010. "Towards a Scientific Concept of Free Will as a Biological Trait: Spontaneous Actions and Decision-Making in Invertebrates." *Proceedings of the Royal Society*, November 25. http://rspb.royalsocietypublishing.org/content/early/2010/12/14/rspb.2010.2325.full.

Bryant, Levi. 2011. *The Democracy of Objects*. Ann Arbor, Mich.: Open Humanities Press.

———. 2013. "I Guess My Ontology Ain't So Flat," in the blog "Larval Subjects," February 14. http://larvalsubjects.wordpress.com/2013/02/14/i-guess-my-ontology-aint-so-flat.

Bryant, Levi, Nick Srnicek, and Graham Harman, eds. 2010. *The Speculative Turn: Continental Materialism and Realism*. Melbourne: re.press.

Chalmers, David. 1995. "Facing Up to the Problem of Consciousness." *Journal of Consciousness Studies* 2, no. 3: 200–219.

———. 1997. *The Conscious Mind: In Search of a Fundamental Theory*. New York: Oxford University Press.

Cobb, John B., and David Ray Griffin. 1976. *Process Theology*. Louisville, Ky.: Westminster John Knox Press.

Cogburn, Jon. 2010. "Brandom on (Sentient) Categorizers versus (Sapient) Inferers." http://drjon.typepad.com/jon_cogburns_blog/2010/03/brandom-on-sentient-categorizers-versus-sapient-inferers.html.

———. 2011. "Some Background on Harman and Speculative Realism." http://www.newappsblog.com/2011/02/some-background-on-harman-and-speculative-realism-and-cool-new-book-series.html.

Coleman, Sam. 2006. "Being Realistic: Why Physicalism May Entail Panexperientialism." In *Consciousness and Its Place in Nature: Does Physicalism Entail Panpsychism?*, edited by Anthony Freeman, 40–52. Charlottesville, Va.: Imprint Academic.

———. 2009. "Mind under Matter." In *Mind That Abides: Panpsychism in the New Millennium*, edited by David Skrbina, 83–108. Philadelphia: John Benjamins.

Coole, Diana, and Samantha Frost. 2010. *New Materialisms: Ontology, Agency, and Politics*. Durham, N.C.: Duke University Press.

Delanda, Manuel. 2002. *Intensive Science and Virtual Philosophy*. New York: Continuum.

———. 2006. *A New Philosophy of Society*. New York: Continuum.

Deleuze, Gilles. 1983. *Nietzsche and Philosophy*. Translated by Hugh Tomlinson. New York: Columbia University Press.

———. 1986. *Cinema 1: The Movement-Image*. Translated by Hugh Tomlinson and Barbara Habberjam. Minneapolis: University of Minnesota Press.

———. 1989. *Cinema 2: The Time-Image*. Translated by Hugh Tomlinson and Robert Galeta. Minneapolis: University of Minnesota Press.

———. 1990. *The Logic of Sense*. Translated by Mark Lester. New York: Columbia University Press.

———. 1993. *The Fold: Leibniz and the Baroque.* Translated by Tom Conley. Minneapolis: University of Minnesota Press.

———. 1994. *Difference and Repetition.* Translated by Paul Patton. New York: Columbia University Press.

Dennett, Daniel. 1988. "Quining Qualia." http://ase.tufts.edu/cogstud/papers/quinqual.htm.

Derrida, Jacques. 1998. *Of Grammatology.* Translated by Gayatri Chakravorty Spivak. Baltimore, Md.: Johns Hopkins University Press.

Dolphijn, Rick, and Iris van der Tuin. 2012. *New Materialism: Interviews & Cartographies.* Ann Arbor, Mich.: Open Humanities.

Dunham, Jeremy. 2009. "Whitehead on the Contingency of Nature's Laws." *Concrescence: The Australasian Journal of Process Thought* 10:35–44.

Freeman, Anthony, ed. 2006. *Consciousness and Its Place in Nature: Does Physicalism Entail Panpsychism?* Charlottesville, Va.: Imprint Academic.

Galloway, Alexander. 2012. *French Theory Today: An Introduction to Possible Futures.* New York: TPSNY/Erudio Editions. http://cultureandcommunication.org/galloway/FTT/French-Theory-Today.pdf.

Gee, Henry, ed. 2007. *Futures from Nature: One Hundred Speculative Fictions from the Pages of the Leading Science Journal.* New York: Tor Books.

Grant, Iain Hamilton. 2006. *Philosophies of Nature after Schelling.* New York: Continuum.

———. 2009. "All Things Think: Panpsychism and the Metaphysics of Nature." In *Mind That Abides: Panpsychism in the New Millennium,* edited by David Skrbina, 283–99. Philadelphia: John Benjamins.

Harman, Graham. 2002. *Tool-Being: Heidegger and the Metaphysics of Objects.* Chicago: Open Court.

———. 2005. *Guerrilla Metaphysics: Phenomenology and the Carpentry of Things.* Chicago: Open Court.

———. 2007a. *Heidegger Explained: From Phenomenon to Thing.* Chicago: Open Court.

———. 2007b. "On Vicarious Causation." *Collapse: Philosophical Research and Development* 2:171–205.

———. 2008. "Intentional Objects for Nonhumans." http://www.europhilosophie.eu/recherche/IMG/pdf/intentional-objects.pdf.

———. 2009a. "OOO: A First Try at Some Parameters." http://doctorzamalek2.wordpress.com/2009/09/04/ooo-a-first-try-at-some-parameters.

———. 2009b. *Prince of Networks: Bruno Latour and Metaphysics.* Melbourne: re.press.

———. 2009c. "Zero-Person and the Psyche." In *Mind That Abides: Panpsychism in the New Millennium,* edited by David Skrbina, 253–82. Philadelphia: John Benjamins.

———. 2010. "I Am Also of the Opinion That Materialism Must Be Destroyed." *Environment and Planning D: Society and Space* 28, no. 5: 772–90.

———. 2011a. *The Quadruple Object*. Winchester, England: Zero Books.

———. 2011b. *Quentin Meillassoux: Philosophy in the Making*. Edinburgh: Edinburgh University Press.

———. 2011c. *Towards Speculative Realism: Essays and Lectures*. Winchester, England: Zero Books.

———. 2012a. *The Third Table*. Ostfildern, Germany: Hatje Kantz.

———. 2012b. "Wolfendale's Piece in the Speculations Issue," in the blog "Object-Oriented Philosophy," September 4.

———. 2013. "The Current State of Speculative Realism." *Speculations* 4:22–28.

James, William. 1890/1983. *The Principles of Psychology*. Cambridge, Mass.: Harvard University Press.

———. 1912/1996. *Essays in Radical Empiricism*. Lincoln: University of Nebraska Press.

Jones, Gwyneth. 2011. "The Universe of Things." In *The Universe of Things*, 48–61. Seattle: Aqueduct Press.

Jones, Judith. 1998. *Intensity: An Essay in Whiteheadian Ontology*. Nashville, Tenn.: Vanderbilt University Press.

Kant, Immanuel. 1998. *Critique of Pure Reason*. Translated by Paul Guyer and Allen W. Wood. New York: Cambridge University Press.

———. 2000. *Critique of Judgment*. Translated by Paul Guyer and Eric Matthews. New York: Cambridge University Press.

Ladyman, James, Don Ross, David Spurrett, and John Gordon Collier. 2007. *Every Thing Must Go: Metaphysics Naturalized*. New York: Oxford University Press.

Laruelle, François. 1999. "A Summary of Non-Philosophy." *Pli* 8:138–48.

———. 2009. *Dictionary of Non-Philosophy*. Translated by Taylor Adkins. http://nsrnicek .googlepages.com/DictionaryNonPhilosophy.pdf.

———. 2011. *The Concept of Non-Photography*. New York: Sequence/Urbanomic.

Latour, Bruno. 1988. *The Pasteurization of France*. Translated by Alan Sheridan and John Law. Cambridge, Mass.: Harvard University Press.

———. 1993. *We Have Never Been Modern*. Translated by Catherine Porter. Cambridge, Mass.: Harvard University Press.

Latty, Tanya, and Madeline Beekman. 2010. "Irrational Decision-Making in an Amoeboid Organism: Transitivity and Context-Dependent Preferences." *Proceedings of the Royal Society B*, published online before print August 11.

Levinas, Emmanuel. 1969. *Totality and Infinity: An Essay on Exteriority*. Translated by Alphonso Lingis. Pittsburgh: Duquesne University Press.

Lewis, David. 1986. *Philosophical Papers II*. New York: Oxford University Press.

Manning, Erin. 2013. *Always More Than One: Individuation's Dance*. Durham, N.C.: Duke University Press.

McGinn, Colin. 2006. "Hard Questions: Comments on Galen Strawson." In *Consciousness and Its Place in Nature: Does Physicalism Entail Panpsychism?*, edited by Anthony Freeman, 90–99. Charlottesville, Va.: Imprint Academic.

McLuhan, Marshall. 1962. *The Gutenberg Galaxy: The Making of Typographic Man.* Toronto: University of Toronto Press.

———. 1964/1994. *Understanding Media: The Extensions of Man.* Cambridge, Mass.: MIT Press.

McLuhan, Marshall, and Quentin Fiore. 1967. *The Medium Is the Message.* New York: Bantam.

Meillassoux, Quentin. 2008. *After Finitude: An Essay on the Necessity of Contingency.* Translated by Ray Brassier. New York: Continuum.

———. 2012. "Iteration, Reiteration, Repetition: A Speculative Analysis of the Meaningless Sign." http://oursecretblog.com/txt/QMpaperApr12.pdf.

Merleau-Ponty, Maurice. 2002. *Phenomenology of Perception.* Translated by Colin Smith. New York: Routledge.

Metzinger, Thomas. 2004. *Being No One: The Self-Model Theory of Subjectivity.* Cambridge, Mass.: MIT Press.

Molnar, George. 2007. *Powers: A Study in Metaphysics.* New York: Oxford University Press.

Morton, Timothy. 2011. "AI, Anti-AI vs OOO, Enaction." http://ecologywithoutnature.blogspot.com/2011/05/ai-anti-ai-vs-ooo-enaction.html.

———. 2013. *Realist Magic: Objects, Ontology, Causality.* Ann Arbor, Mich.: Open Humanities Press.

Mullarkey, John. 2006. *Post-Continental Philosophy: An Outline.* New York: Continuum.

———. 2012. "Can We Think Democratically? Laruelle and the 'Arrogance' of Non-Philosophy." http://www.thelondongraduateschool.co.uk/thoughtpiece/can-we-think-democratically-laruelle-and-the-arrogance-of-non-philosophy.

Mumford, Stephen, and Rani Lill Anjum. 2011. *Getting Causes from Powers.* New York: Oxford University Press.

Nagel, Thomas. 1991. *Mortal Questions.* New York: Cambridge University Press.

Negarestani, Reza. 2008. *Cyclonopedia: Complicity with Anonymous Materials.* Melbourne: re.press.

Nietzsche, Friedrich. 1997. *On the Genealogy of Morality.* Edited by Keith Ansell Pearson. Translated by Carol Diethe. New York: Cambridge University Press.

———. 1999. *The Birth of Tragedy and Other Writings.* Edited by Raymond Geuss and Ronald Speirs. Translated by Ronald Speirs. New York: Cambridge University Press.

Olson, Charles. 1987. *The Collected Poems of Charles Olson: Excluding the Maximus Poems.* Edited by George Butterick. Berkeley: University of California Press.

Peckham, Morse. 1979. *Explanation and Power: The Control of Human Behavior.* Minneapolis: University of Minnesota Press.

Pulos, C. E. 1954. *The Deep Truth: A Study of Shelley's Skepticism*. Lincoln: University of Nebraska Press.

Roden, David. 2013. "Nature's Dark Domain: An Argument for a Naturalized Phenomenology." *Royal Institute of Philosophy Supplement* 72 (July): 169–88.

Rucker, Rudy. 2006. "Mind Is a Universally Distributed Quality." http://www.edge.org/q2006/q06_3.html#rucker.

———. 2007. "Panpsychism Proved." In *Futures from Nature: One Hundred Speculative Fictions from the Pages of the Leading Science Journal*, edited by Henry Gee, 248–50. New York: Tor Books.

Savarese, Ralph James, and Emily Thorton Savarese, eds. 2010. "Autism and the Concept of Neurodiversity." Special issue, *Disability Studies Quarterly* 30:1.

Seager, William. 2006. "The 'Intrinsic Nature' Argument for Panpsychism." In *Consciousness and Its Place in Nature: Does Physicalism Entail Panpsychism?*, edited by Anthony Freeman, 129–45. Charlottesville, Va.: Imprint Academic.

Sellars, Wilfrid. 1997. *Empiricism and the Philosophy of Mind*. Cambridge, Mass.: Harvard University Press.

Shaviro, Steven. 2003. *Connected, or, What It Means to Live in the Network Society*. Minneapolis: University of Minnesota Press.

———. 2009. *Without Criteria: Kant, Whitehead, Deleuze, and Aesthetics*. Cambridge, Mass.: MIT Press.

———, ed. 2011. *Cognition and Decision in Nonhuman Biological Organisms*. Ann Arbor, Mich.: Open Humanities Press.

Simondon, Gilbert. 2005. *L'individuation à la lumière des notions de forme et d'information*. Grenoble, France: Million.

Skrbina, David. 2005. *Panpsychism in the West*. Cambridge, Mass.: MIT Press.

———, ed. 2009. *Mind That Abides: Panpsychism in the New Millennium*. Philadelphia: John Benjamins.

Sobchack, Vivian. 1992. *The Address of the Eye: A Phenomenology of Film Experience*. Princeton, N.J.: Princeton University Press.

Stengers, Isabelle. 2009. "Thinking with Deleuze and Whitehead: A Double Test." In *Deleuze, Whitehead, Bergson: Rhizomatic Connections*, edited by Keith Robinson, 28–44. New York: Palgrave Macmillan.

———. 2011. *Thinking with Whitehead: A Free and Wild Creation of Concepts*. Translated by Michael Chase. Cambridge, Mass.: Harvard University Press.

Sterling, Bruce. 2005. *Shaping Things*. Cambridge, Mass.: MIT Press.

Strawson, Galen. 2006. "Realistic Monism: Why Physicalism Entails Panpsychism." In *Consciousness and Its Place in Nature: Does Physicalism Entail Panpsychism?*, edited by Anthony Freeman, 3–31. Charlottesville, Va.: Imprint Academic.

Thacker, Eugene. 2011. *In the Dust of This Planet*. Winchester, England: Zero Books.

Trewavas, Anthony. 2003. "Aspects of Plant Intelligence." *Annals of Botany* 92:1–20.

Trewavas, Anthony, and František Baluška. 2011. "The Ubiquity of Consciousness." *EMBO Reports* 12 (18 November): 1221–25.

Tulving, Endel. 1985. "Memory and Consciousness." *Canadian Psychology/Psychologie Canadienne* 26:1.

Whitehead, Alfred North. 1920/2004. *The Concept of Nature*. Amherst, N.Y.: Prometheus Books. [*CN*].

———. 1925/1967. *Science and the Modern World*. New York: Free Press. [*SMW*].

———. 1926/1996. *Religion in the Making*. New York: Fordham University Press. [*RM*].

———. 1929/1978. *Process and Reality*. New York: Free Press. [*PR*].

———. 1933/1967. *Adventures of Ideas*. New York: Free Press. [*AI*].

———. 1938. *Modes of Thought*. New York: Free Press. [*MT*].

———. 1948. *Science and Philosophy*. New York: Philosophical Library. [*SP*].

Wittgenstein, Ludwig. 1922/2001. *Tractatus Logico-Philosophicus*. Translated by D. F. Pears and B. F. McGuinness. New York: Routledge.

———. 1953. *Philosophical Investigations*, 4th ed. Translated by G. E. M. Anscombe, P. M. S. Hacker, and Joachim Schulte. Madden, Mass.: Wiley-Blackwell.

Wolfendale, Pete. 2009. "Phenomenology, Discourse, and Their Objects." http://deontol ogistics.wordpress.com/2009/12/20/phenomenology-discourse-and-their-objects.

———. 2010. "Brandom on Ethics." http://deontologistics.wordpress.com/2010/02/27/ brandom-and-ethics.

———. 2012. "Not So Humble Pie." http://deontologistics.files.wordpress.com/2012/04/ wolfendale-nyt.pdf.

Woodard, Ben. 2012. *On an Ungrounded Earth: Towards a New Geophilosophy*. New York: Punctum Books.

Žižek, Slavoj. 1993. *Tarrying with the Negative: Kant, Hegel, and the Critique of Ideology*. Durham, N.C.: Duke University Press.

———. 2012. *Less Than Nothing: Hegel and the Shadow of Dialectical Materialism*. New York: Verso.

INDEX

actants, paradoxes of nonhuman, 48
actualism, Whitehead and Harman
linked by, 34–35, 37
Adventures of Ideas (Whitehead), 2, 16,
17, 34; conversion of conceptual
oppositions into aesthetic design of
"patterned contrasts" in, 19–20, 34; on
Truth and Beauty, 19–20, 41–42
aesthetic(s), 12, 13; of attraction and
repulsion, 54; of the beautiful versus
of the sublime, 41–43; Derrida on,
judgment as citational or iterable,
151; experience as asymmetrical, 63;
feeling object for its own sake, 53;
Harman on, 13, 30, 156; Harman's
aestheticist revision of Kant, 70, 138,
146, 148; Kantian aesthetic idea,
154–55; Kant's discussion of, 148–56;
Kant's notion of aesthetic disinterest,
151–53; as key to causality, 138,
144–48; metamorphosis and, 53–54;
as mode of contact between beings,
61; noncorrelational thought as, 133;
singularity and supplementarity
of things and, 53; speculative, 156;
twentieth-century, 43; twenty-first
century revaluation of, 20, 43–44;
understanding other entities through
aesthetic semblances, 91; values of
nature, 59; Whitehead on aesthetic
design of "patterned contrasts,"

19–20, 34; Whitehead's aestheticized
account of ethics, 24, 25–26
After Finitude (Meillassoux), 67, 72, 75
Agamben, Giorgio, 152; on whatever
being, 152
agential realism, 11
aisthesis, 12, 134–56; causation, views
of, 33, 37, 138, 139–48, 151; Kantian
aesthetics, 133, 148–56. *See also*
perception
"Aleutian" cycle, Jones's, 45, 46. *See also*
"Universe of Things, The"
alien phenomenology, 92
allure: as engine for change, 53; as form
of knowledge, 91; Harman's aesthetics
of, 42, 43, 53–54, 59, 60, 91, 138;
metamorphosis in contrast to, 53–54,
59, 60; of nature, 59
allusion: Harman on, 70, 91, 136, 144,
145, 151; understanding other entities
by, 91, 136
"Analytic of Concepts" (Kant), 153–54
"Analytic of the Beautiful" (Kant), 148–56
animality: nonhuman versus human
animals, human exceptionalism and,
87; rupture between human thought
and, Meillassoux's assumption of,
126–27. *See also* nonhuman entities
animate-inanimate distinction, 62
Anjum, Rani Lill, 142; realist approach to
causality, 143, 144, 145–46

antecedence, Grant on, 70
anthropocentrism, 60–61, 72–73, 91;
Bennett on, 61; established on basis
of its own critical self-reflexivity,
Kant and, 72; Harman's rejection of,
while affirming irreducible finitude,
135–36, 137; of Meillassoux, 125–28,
135; persistence of panpsychism
as kind of countertendency to, 86;
speculative realists questioning of,
1, 8, 9; undermined by Darwin, 72;
undermined in Jones's "The Universe
of Things," 45–46
anthropomorphism, 90–91
antinomies, 19
antirealism, twentieth-century continental philosophy premised on, 5
appropriation: destructive, life as process
of, 15–16, 24; self-enjoyment arising
out of process of, 15–16, 21
Aristotle, 8, 18; fourfold classification of
causes, 139
atomism, 3, 23, 34–35, 104
autistic modes of thought, 132
autopoiesis, 89; operations of autopoietic
system, 144–45

Badiou, Alain, 74, 111, 120, 122
Baluška, František, 88
Barad, Karen, 11, 62, 99
Barthes, Roland, 120
Bataille, Georges, 70
Bateson, Gregory, 145
beauty: aesthetics of the beautiful versus
of the sublime, 41–43; as appropriate
to a world of relations, 42; Kant on,
148–56; Kant on, definition of, 154;
Metzinger on, 133; twentieth-century
aesthetics disregard for, 43; Whitehead on Truth and Beauty, 19–20,
41–42, 78. See also aesthetic(s)
becoming: being subordinated to, 3; as
generic notion, 8; metamorphosis,
53–54, 60; as multiplicity of discrete

"occasions," 3–4; processes of, 2–3, 4,
8, 35, 102
Beekman, Madeline, 127
behavior, inferring existence of inner
experience from, 94–97
behaviorism, 96
being: Agamben on whatever being, 152;
Deleuze's doctrine of univocity of,
150; hierarchy of, 29; subordinated
to becoming, 3. See also thought and
being
Benjamin, Walter, 20
Bennett, Jane, 52, 99; on anthropocentrism, 61; on vital materialism, 11,
48, 62
Bergson, Henri, 11, 22, 125, 131
Berkeley, George, 66; origins of correlationism in, 108–9, 110
Bhaskar, Roy, 71
bifurcation of nature, 65–66; Brassier's
reconceptualization of, 120, 123;
Meillassoux's validation of, 74,
115–16, 123; into phenomenal versus
scientific registers of existence, 114;
Western philosophy reinforcing, 3, 8,
114; Whitehead's quest to overcome,
1–3, 8, 114
Blamauer, Michael, 86
blind emotion, as primitive form of
experience, 79–80
blind thought, 130
Bogost, Ian, 5, 27, 92
Bradley, F. H., 94
Braidotti, Rosi, 11
Brandom, Robert, 90; on sentience–
sapience distinction, 87
Brassier, Ray, 2, 5, 65, 73, 83, 119; assumption about matter being passive
and inert, 77; on Berkeley, 108–9;
on correlationism, 6, 108–9, 120–22;
"eliminativist" versions of speculative realism, 91, 121; metaphysical
speculation based on physical science,
10; physicalist revision of Kantian

distinction between phenomena and noumena, 70–71; reconceptualization of bifurcation of nature, 120, 123; reductionist dismissal of subjective and phenomenal qualities, 120–22; similarity/contrast to Meillassoux, 120, 122–24; transcendental realism of, 71, 121–22; truth of extinction, 74–75

Braver, Lee, 5, 67

Brembs, Bjorn, 126

Brentano, Franz, 80

British empiricism, 58

Brown, Spencer, 145

Bryant, Levi, 5, 6, 9, 10–11, 27, 70, 71, 74, 89, 109, 120, 121; "democracy of objects," 60; on exo-qualities as distinct from endo-qualities, 116; on relational theory, 31–32; theory of autopoiesis, 89, 144–45

Cantor, Georg, 69, 122

"Categories of the Understanding" (Kant), 140, 155

causal efficacy: in form of "vague terrors," 59; perception in mode of, 28–29; romanticism in, 56–57, 59; Whitehead's notion of, 55–60

causation: aesthetics as key to causality, 138, 144–48; Aristotle's fourfold classification of causes, modern rejection of, 139; efficient, in physical science, 138; Hume on, 139, 140, 142, 146; Kant on, 139–40, 146; Lewis on, 139, 141, 142, 146; Meillassoux's reversal of Kant's analysis, 140–41, 146; Molnar on, 142–43, 144; Morton on, 138–39; Mumford and Anjum on, 143, 144, 145–46; nonanthropocentric, realist analysis of, 141–43, 144, 145–46; in object-oriented ontology, 138–39, 144–45; as occult influence, 138, 148; separation of the causal from the ontological, 142; vicarious, Harman on, 33, 37, 56, 70, 118, 138, 146, 148, 151

Chalmers, David, 63; on "hard problem" of consciousness, 96

change: allure as engine of, for Harman, 53; critiques of Whitehead's relational theory in light of, 31–32, 37; Whitehead's account of "perpetually perishing" world, 32, 36, 38, 40; will to, 89. *See also* creativity; novelty

Cinema (Deleuze), 130–31

closure, operational, 144–45

Cobb, John B., 4

Cogburn, Jon, 67, 87

cognitive judgment, for Kant, 152–53

Coleman, Sam, 100; foundational ontological principle, 102–3, 104

Collier, John Gordon, 103

common sense: breaking away from, 9–10; correlationism and, 66

commonsense realism, 110

common world, distinct entities as elements of, 60

complexity theory, 62

conatus, 89

conceptual initiative, 89

concern: connection between self-enjoyment and, 15–16; to denote "affective tone," 16; distinction between self-enjoyment and, 14–15, 16, 17; publicity of, 17; Quaker sense of term, 14, 16. *See also* self-enjoyment and concern

concrescence, Whitehead's definition of, 35

Connected (Shaviro), 33–34

consciousness: Chalmers on "hard problem" of, 96; as essentially representational, Metzinger on, 118; James on, 78; Morton on, 79; neural correlates of, search for, 100; and thing, efforts to overcome duality of, 131; Whitehead on, 79

contact at a distance, 147–48; prehension as, 118

contact between beings, aesthetics as
mode of, 61
contingency, Meillassoux on: intellectual
intuition as affirmation of pure
contingency, 113, 124–25, 127, 130;
of Kantian correlation of thought
and being, 69, 75; of "laws of nature,"
122–23; necessity of contingency, 10,
100, 134, 140, 146
continuity, Bergsonian, 22–23
contrasts: converting conceptual
oppositions into patterned, 19–20, 34;
differences between Whitehead and
Harman as, 34, 41, 43
Coole, Diana, 11
Copernicus, 45
co-propriation *(Zusammengehörigkei)* of
man and being, Heidegger on, 73
correlationism, 57; bifurcation of nature
and, 65–66; Brassier on, 6, 108–9,
120–22; common sense and, 66;
domination of Western philosophy,
6, 7–8; established on basis of its own
critical self-reflexivity, Kant and, 72;
"exteriority" to thought posited by,
109; founding premise of, 140; "givenness" of world to us, 109–10; Harman's
opposition to, 6, 30, 110; Heidegger's
readiness-to-hand concept as way
out of, 49; Husserl's modified, 109;
Kantian aesthetics preceding, 148–56;
Meillassoux on, 6, 7, 8–9; Meillassoux
on escaping, 112–13, 119, 124–25;
Meillassoux on origins of, 108–10;
Meillassoux on twin "fundamental
decisions" of, 128; Meillassoux's definition of, 111–13, 123–24; Merleau-
Ponty's modified, 109; primordial
"vector feeling" as raw material of, 80;
rejection of, by speculative realists,
5–10, 63, 65, 66; self-reflexivity of, 6–7,
110; of Shelley's "Mont Blanc," subversion of, 58–59; starting point of, 68–69;
stepping outside circle of, 68–75;

Whitehead's opposition to, basis of,
30. *See also* noncorrelational thought;
thought and being
creativity, Whitehead on, 101; "creative
advance," 40; as highest value, 4, 8
critical realism, 71
Critique of Judgment (Kant), 148

dark materialism, 83
dark vitalism, 83
Darwin, Charles, 45, 72, 91
decision: as act of selection, 39–40; novelty arising from act of positive, 39–40;
philosophical, Laruelle on, 128, 129
deconstruction, as negatively correlationist, 7
default metaphysics, 66, 67
Delanda, Manuel, 99, 143; reconstruction
of Deleuze's transcendental empiricism, 71–72
Deleuze, Gilles, 4, 35, 37, 60, 108, 111,
121, 125; on apprehension of time
in Kant, 155; approach to noncorrelational thought, 130–32, 133;
doctrine of univocity of being, 150; on
historical crisis of psychology, 130–31;
object of encounter of, Kantian
"aesthetic idea" prefiguring, 154–55;
transcendental empiricism, 71–72; on
Whitehead inventing mannerism in
philosophy, 18; Whitehead's processes
and becoming linked with, 35
democracy: basis in common fact of
value experience, 25; of fellow creatures, 60, 63; of objects, 11, 60, 63
Dennett, Daniel, 93–94; eliminativism
of, 93, 98
Derrida, Jacques, 70, 120; aesthetic judgment as citational or iterable, 151; on
deconstruction, 7; Kantian project
radicalized and completed by, 9
Descartes, René, 9, 18, 28, 87, 115; bifurcation of nature and, 2, 3; "clear and
distinct" ideas, 55, 98; dualism and

reification as most problematic parts of argument of, 99

destructive appropriation, life as process of, 15–16, 24

Diderot, Denis, 125

disinterest, Kant's notion of aesthetic, 151–53

dispositions, 80

Divine Inexistence, The (Meillassoux), 75, 125

dogmatism, 7, 9, 69

Dolphijn, Rick, 11

dormant objects, Harman on, 147

double intuition, 32–33, 34

Drummond, William, 58

economy, 13

Eddington, Arthur, 102

efficient causation of physical science, 138

eliminativism, 12, 61; anticorrelationism leading to radical, 73–75; of Brassier, 91, 121; of Dennett, 93, 98; human exceptionalism presupposed in, 77; persistence of nonhuman values as problem for, 91; rejection of, 63; speculative realists combining extreme tendencies of both panpsychism and, 83–84; Strawson on, 82

emergence, Strawson's rejection of brute, 100

emotion: blind, as primitive form of experience, 79–80; concern and self-enjoyment as movements of, 16. *See also* feeling(s)

empiricism, 69; British, 58; transcendental, 71–72

endo-qualities, 116, 117

enjoyment. *See* self-enjoyment and concern

entelechy-infused life and inorganic matter, vitalist distinction between, 62

epistemism, 119, 121, 123

epistemological thesis of speculative realism, 68

epistemology, 3, 13, 92; deprivileging, 3; Harman's epistemological argument, 105–6, 107, 118, 137; Hume's epistemological doubt about causality, 140

equality, ontological, 29–31

essentialism, 18

ethics: encounter with the Other and demands of ethical transcendence, Levinas on, 21–22, 25; Whitehead's aestheticized account of, 24, 25–26

exceptionalism, human, 75; eliminativist arguments presupposing, 77; Harman's argument against, 80; insistence on centrality of linguistic forms and, 87; Meillassoux's anthropocentrism and, 125–28

existentialism, 121

exo-qualities, 116, 117

experience: blind emotion as primitive form of, 79–80; common fact of value experience, Whitehead's vision of, 25, 77–78, 89–90; described by but not accounted for by physics, 102; first-person, versus third-person, objective knowledge, 93; inner sensations, 92–98; inner sensations, Wittgenstein on, 92–95, 97; James's characterization of, 78–79; language and inner, 95, 96–97; nonconscious, 79; of nonhuman others, Nagel on, 91–92, 95–96, 102; ontological status of, 92–93, 94; panpsychism as necessary consequence of respecting self-evidence of phenomenal, 101; primordial, 97; as vague and indistinct, Whitehead on, 97

extensive continuum, 23

"exteriority" to thought, correlationism on, 109

extinction, Brassier's truth of, 74–75

fact and value, entwining of, 24–25, 26

fear of liveliness of things, 48

hidden properties, Harman's doctrine of, 30, 37–38, 39
hierarchy of being, 29
horror of philosophy, Thacker's, 84
human exceptionalism, 75, 77, 80, 87, 125–28
Hume, David, 9, 58, 80, 90, 98; on causality, 139, 140, 142, 146; on causality, Meillassoux's reversion to, 140–41, 146
Humean skepticism, crisis of, 65–66
Husserl, Edmund, 54, 124; efforts to "overcome" duality of consciousness and thing, 131; modified correlationism of, 109
hylemorphic schema, 153

idealism: confrontation of materialism and, in historical crisis of psychology, 131; panpsychism's rebuke to, 86; qualia in, 94; of Shelley in "Mont Blanc," 57–58; subjective, 110; transcendental, 71
"Immortality" (Whitehead), 17, 19
immortality, objective, 36
indirect causation. See vicarious causation
individuation, 89
information processing, representationalist, 131
inner sensations, 88, 92–98
intellectual intuition of the absolute, Meillassoux's noncorrelational thought as, 113–14, 124–25, 127, 130, 134–35
intentionality: aesthetic encounter without phenomenological, 153; detranscendentalizing, 81, 82; doubled or supplemented by self-reflexivity, 110; of perception and sentience, phenomenological assumption of, 124; physical, 80–81, 82
interiority, self-reflexive, 110
interrelatedness of all things, 4, 5
intrinsic natures, 102–4; as gap in physics, 102–3; Seager and Harman on, 103–4

intuition(s): Kant's definition of beauty as, 154; Kant's sensible, 114; Meillassoux's intellectual, 113–14, 124–25, 127, 130, 134–35; about world, Whitehead and Harman on, 32–33, 34
irreflective thought, 130
isolation, living world of Aleutians in Jones's "The Universe of Things" versus human, 46, 47

James, William, 15, 60; call for philosophy that does justice to conjunctive relations, 40; deliberate project of "depsychologization" of experience, 78–79; opposition to "neo-Kantian" doctrine, 79
Johnson, Samuel, 66, 110
Jones, Gwyneth, 45–49, 51, 57, 59; "Aleutian" cycle, 45, 46. See also "Universe of Things, The"
Jones, Judith, 4

Kant, Immanuel, 3, 8, 9, 108; on aesthetics, 133, 148–56; analysis of paralogisms, 69; antinomies of, 19; assertion of unknowability, 68; on causality, 139–40, 146; on causality, as Category of the Understanding, 140; centrality of "human-world relation" assumed by, 135; "Copernican revolution" in philosophy, 6, 72; on existence of God, 75, 152; Kantian catastrophe, 68–69; on nonhuman Real, 67–68; noumena and phenomena, 2, 30, 70, 135; on perception, 117; philosophy of finitude, circumventing, 134–36, 149; resolution of crisis of Humean skepticism, 65–66; schemata, 154; on self-reflexive interiority, 110; on sensible intuition, 114; on space and time, 155; speculative realists' revisions of Kantian settlement, 67, 69–75, 78, 138, 146, 148; on taste, 43; transcendental argument, 6–7, 28, 70, 71, 110

Kasparov, Garry, 45
knowledge: aesthetic contact outside,
148; by allusion, Harman on, 91, 136;
external, structural, and relational,
through physics, 103; finitude of, 135–
37; first-person experience versus
third-person objective, 93; inability
to equate object with or reduce it to,
105–6; of inner sensations, Wittgenstein on, 94–95; scientific, leading
to thought's recognition of its own
extinction, 122

Lacan, Jacques, 120
Lacanian psychoanalysis, 7
Ladyman, James, 103, 105
language: human exceptionalism and
centrality of, 87; inner experience
and, 95, 96–97
Laruelle, François: nonphilosophy of,
128–30, 133; on photography's "radi-
cal critique" of perception, 130, 132
Latour, Bruno, 4, 11, 28, 48, 117
Latty, Tanya, 127
Leibniz, Gottfried Wilhelm von, 18, 68,
88, 103
Levinas, Emmanuel, 12; comparing
Whitehead with, 20–27
Lévi-Strauss, Claude, 120
Lewis, David, 143; on causal connections,
139, 141, 142, 146
Locke, John, 2, 115
Lovecraft, H. P., 147
Lucretius, physics of, 88, 102, 103
Luhmann, Niklas, 144; theory of autopoi-
esis, 145
lures for feeling, Whitehead on, 54–55,
154

Mallarmé, Stephane, 12
"manifest image" and "scientific image,"
distinction between, 120
mannerist philosophy, 18
Manning, Erin, 132

materialism: confrontation of idealism
and, in historical crisis of psychology,
131; dark, 83; mechanistic, 62; new, 1,
5, 11, 99, 100; vitalist, 11, 48, 62, 63
mathematics/science: Galloway on
mathematical formalization as indispensable component of "post-Fordist
modernity," 119–20; Meillassoux's
recourse to, 10, 115, 119, 120, 122–23;
noncorrelational access to reality
through, dispute over, 119. See also
physical science; physics
mathematization of nature, 74, 115
Maturana, 144
McGinn, Colin, 86
McLuhan, Marshall, 46, 59; on media as
"extensions of man," 51, 52
mechanistic materialism, 62
media as "extensions of man," McLuhan
on, 51, 52
Meillassoux, Quentin, 2, 5–6, 49, 65, 66,
73–74, 83; absolute rationalism of,
123–24, 125, 135; on aim of speculative realism, 68; anthropocentrism
of, 125–28, 135; assumption of
passive and inert matter, 77; on
contingency (facticity) of Kantian
correlation of thought and being,
69, 75; on contingency of "laws of
nature," 122–23; on correlationism, 6,
7, 8–9; on correlationism, definition,
111–13, 123–24; on correlationism,
origins, 108–10; on correlationism,
twin "fundamental decisions" of, 128;
"eliminativist" versions of speculative
realism, 91; on escaping correlationism, 112–13, 119, 124–25; extermination of sentience and perception, 113,
115, 123; on intellectual intuition of
the absolute, 113–14, 124–25, 127,
130, 134–35; on Kant, 68–69, 72, 75,
134; on mathematization of nature,
74, 115; necessity of contingency,
notion of, 10, 100, 134, 140, 146;

noncorrelational thought of, 113–14, 119, 124–25, 127, 134–35; objections to principle of sufficient reason, 76, 123; opposition to phenomenology, 123, 124; "origin of pure novelty" out of nothing, 100–101; paradoxical task of speculative philosophy for, 111, 113; parallels between Laruelle's approach to standard philosophy and anticorrelationist critique of, 128–30; recourse to mathematics, 10, 115, 119, 120, 122–23; rehabilitation of life and thought in *The Divine Inexistence*, 75; rejection of subjectivity, 73, 123–26; reversal of Kant's analysis of causality and reversion to "Hume's Problem," 140–41, 146; similarity/contrast to Brassier, 120, 122–24; thesis of radical emergence of thought out of nothingness, 82; validation of bifurcation of nature, 74, 115–16, 123

mentality: diffuse and widespread, 98; extension beyond the human, arguments against, 87; extension beyond the human, panpsychism and, 85–90; multiple modes of thought, 127–28; preassumed, in Strawson's argument for panpsychism, 98–99, 101

Merleau-Ponty, Maurice, 108, 124, 130; modified correlationism of, 109; on self-reflexive interiority, 110

metamorphosis, 53–54, 60; in nature, 59

metaphysical subject, Wittgenstein on, 7

metaphysics: default, 66, 67; difference between science and, Brassier on, 121; of Harmon, 28; beyond human sphere, 8; metaphysical problem of ubiquitous relations, 33–34; positive programs of metaphysical speculation, differences between, 10–11; restoring dignity of, 5

Metzinger, Thomas, 63, 95; on beauty, 133; on consciousness as essentially representational, 118

Mind That Abides (Skrbina), 83

modernity, displacements and decenterings of human throughout, 45

Modes of Thought (Whitehead), 2, 14; polarity between self-enjoyment and concern as patterned contrast in, 20; rhetorical difference between *Process and Reality* and, 17

Molnar, George: on physical intentionality, 80; realist account of cause and effect proposed by, 142–43, 144

"Mont Blanc" (Shelley), 57–59; subject–object binary posited in, 58

moral judgment, for Kant, 152–53

morals, 25

Morton, Timothy, 5, 27; on causality, 138–39; on consciousness, 79

Mullarkey, John, 129, 130

Mumford, Stephen, 142; realist approach to causality, 143, 144, 145–46

Nagel, Thomas, 85; on experience of nonhuman others, 91–92, 95–96, 102

naïve realism, 7, 66

naturalism, Meillassoux's rejection of, 123

nature: aesthetic values of, 59; contingency of "laws of nature," Meillassoux on, 122–23; interpenetration and "cumulation" of things in, 59–60; mathematization of, 74, 115; romantic idea of, 56–60. *See also* bifurcation of nature

nature philosophy, Grant's, 11

Negarestani, Reza, 83

neutrino, public and private elements of, 104–5

new materialism, 1, 11

Newton, Isaac, 103

Nietzsche, Friedrich, 115, 123, 125; criticism of Kant's notion of aesthetic disinterest, 151; justification of world as aesthetic phenomenon, 156

noncorrelational sentience, 128–33

combining extreme tendencies of both eliminativism and, 83–84; Strawson's argument for, 86, 98–102
"Panpsychism Proved" (Rucker), 85
"Paralogisms of Pure Reason" (Kant), 69
Peckham, Morse, 43
perception, 38; as exclusively relational activity, Harman on, 146–47; intentionality of, assumed in phenomenology, 124; Kant on, 117; Meillassoux's extermination of, 113, 115, 123; in mode of causal efficacy, 28–29; multifarious forms of, 127; natural, Deleuze on movies' break with, 131; as nonrepresentational process of continual feedback, response, and adjustment, 118; photography's "radical critique" of, 130, 132
phenomenology, 2, 5, 112, 114; alien, 92; assumption of intentionality of perception and sentience in, 124; correlationist assumptions in, 7; Meillassoux's opposition to, 123, 124
philosophical Decision, Laruelle on, 128, 129
Philosophical Investigations (Wittgenstein), 94
philosophy: Kant's "Copernican revolution" in, 6, 72; Laruelle's approach to standard, 128–30; love of wisdom without claim to actual wisdom, 136; mannerist, 18; Thacker's horror of, 84. *See also* speculative realism; Western philosophy
photography, Laruelle on: "immanence-of-vision" of photograph, 132; "radical critique" of perception by, 130, 132
physical intentionality, 80–81, 82
physical science: Brassier's transcendental realism revising Kant's transcendental idealism and, 71; efficient causation described by, 138; escaping from correlationism through, Brassier's use of, 120–22; Meillassoux's use of, 122, 123;

metaphysical speculation based on, 10; understanding meaninglessness of existence through, 121–22
physics, 99, 100, 102–3; intrinsic nature as gap in, panpsychism's effort to fill, 102–3; of Lucretius, 88, 102, 103; Whitehead's philosophy of process in relation to, 102
post-Fordism, qualities derived from math under, 119–20
posthuman, emergence of, 5
posthuman era, in Jones's "The Universe of Things," 46–49
poststructuralism, radical, 7
potentiality: Harman's rejection of, 37; proposition and, 54–55
powers: causal, realist approaches to, 142–43; of entities beyond human sphere, 8; as intrinsic properties of objects bearing them, 142, 143–44
prehension(s), 72; as contact-at-a-distance, 118; defined, 29; entities constituted by integrating multiple, 29–30; revaluation and, 38; translation of datum into different form, 38–39
presentational immediacy, 28, 55–56
"primary qualities" of matter, 115–17; distinctions made between secondary qualities and, 74, 115–17; placing in same category as secondary qualities, 117–19; problem of accessing, 116–17
primordial experience, 97
privacy: publicity and, antithesis between, 17, 35–36, 104–7; of self-enjoyment, 17, 36
probabilistic reasoning, 69
Process and Reality (Whitehead), 2, 16, 60, 97; grand vision of "God and the World" in, 18–19, 29; objective immortality in, 36; use of term *self-enjoyment* in, 17
processes of becoming, 2–3, 4, 8, 35; giving rise to novelty, 4; in relation to physics, 102

process theologians, 4

proposition: potentiality and, 54–55; Whitehead's definition of, 54

psychic additions, 115

psychoanalysis, Lacanian, 7

psychology, Deleuze on historical crisis of, 130–31

publicity and privacy: antithesis between, 17, 35–36, 104–7; distinction of reason as distinction between, 106

publicity of concern, 17

Pulos, C. E., 58

qualia (inner sensations), 88, 93–98

quantum theory, 99

radical eliminativism, 73–75

radical immanence, Laruelle's affirmation of, 129, 130

radical poststructuralism, 7

radical relationism, 103–4

Rancière, Jacques, 87

rationalism, 69; Meillassoux's absolute, 123–24, 125, 135

readiness-to-hand (*Zuhandenheit*) concept, 48–49; Harman's tool-being as expansion of, 49–51

Real, the: in Lacanian psychoanalysis, 7; Žižek on, 67

realism: agential, 11; approaches to causality, 142–43, 144, 145–46; commonsense, 110; critical, 71; naïve, 7, 66; of the remainder, neo-Kantian, 67, 68; transcendental, 71, 121–22. *See also* speculative realism

Realist Magic (Morton), 138

reality: as entity without thought, Meillassoux on, 112–13; noncorrelational access to, dispute over whether mathematics and science allow, 119; philosophical Decision and possibility of unitary discourse on, 128; as "totally a-subjective," for Meillassoux, 73

reason: distinction of, as distinction between publicity and privacy, 106;

Kant on limited capacity of human, 134; probabilistic reasoning, 69; sufficient, principle of, 76–77, 100–101, 123

reductionist scientism, 114

relationalism, 107; radical, 103–4

relational theory, 31–32, 37; Bryant on, 31–32; Harman versus Whitehead on, 31–32, 35

relations: beauty as appropriate to world of, 42; James's call for philosophy that does justice to conjunctive, 40; ubiquitous, metaphysical problem of, 33–34

remainder, neo-Kantian realism of the, 67, 68

representationalist information processing, 131

responsibility, valuation and, 25

revaluation, 24; prehension leading to, 38

romanticism: romantic idea of Nature, 56–60; in Whitehead's notion of causal efficacy, 56–57, 59

Rorty, Richard, 87

Ross, Don, 103, 105

Rucker, Rudy, 85–86, 88

Russell, Bertrand, 102

sapience-sentience distinction, 87

Savarese, Emily Thorton, 132

Savarese, Ralph James, 132

Schelling, F. W. J., 35, 70, 125

schema, hylemorphic, 153

Schopenhauer, Arthur, 125

Science and the Modern World (Whitehead), 57–60

"scientific image" and "manifest image," distinction between, 120

scientism, 116; of Brassier, 120–22; qualia in, 94; reductionist, 114. *See also* mathematics/science; physical science

Seager, William, 103–4

secondary qualities: distinctions made between primary qualities and, 74, 115–17; placing in same category as primary qualities, 117–19; problem of accessing, 116–17

selection, decision as act of, 39–40

self-causation, ontological principle and, 76

self-enjoyment and concern, Whitehead on, 14–26; in antithesis between publicity and privacy, 17; comparing Whitehead with Levinas, 20–27; connection between, 15–16; distinction between, 14–15, 16, 17; mannerist philosophy and multiplicity and mutability of ways of enjoyment, 18; privacy of self-enjoyment, 17, 36

self-evidence of phenomenal experience, panpsychism as necessary consequence of respecting, 101

self-reflexivity: of correlationism, 6–7, 110; self-reflexive interiority, 110; of thought, Kant's Copernican revolution in philosophy establishing, 72

Sellars, Wilfrid, 2, 120; distinction between "manifest image" and "scientific image," 120

sensationalism: of Shelley's "Mont Blanc," subversion of, 58–59; Whitehead's definition of, 58

sensations: aesthetic, 133; beauty and excess of, 154; inner, 88, 92–98; Meillassoux's downgrading of, 73, 74, 113, 115; presentational immediacy of, 28; vicarious, 151. *See also* feeling(s); perception; sentience

sentience: active self-valuation of all entities, 89–91; different degrees and forms of, 127; intentionality of, assumed in phenomenology, 124; involved in Kantian aesthetic judgment, 153–54; Meillassoux's extermination of, 113, 115, 123; noncorrelational, 128–33; of nonhuman entities, biological research on, 126, 127–28; as nonintentional and noncognitive, Deleuze on, 131–32; sentience-sapience distinction, 87;

Strawson's insistence on presence of, 101

Shaviro, Steven, 4, 9, 63, 72, 88, 126

Shelley, Percy Bysshe, 57–59

Simondon, Gilbert, 35, 89, 153

singularity: of beauty, 149; of things, aesthetics and, 53; universality and, 149–54

skepticism, 69; crisis of Humean, 65–66

Skrbina, David, 83, 86; on panpsychism, 63, 85

smallism, 100

Sobchack, Vivian, 110

solipsism, problem of, 87

space and time, Kant on, 155

speculative aesthetics, 156

speculative realism, 1, 5–11; aim of, Meillassoux on, 68; basic thesis of, 66–67; combining most extreme tendencies of both panpsychism and eliminativism, 83–84; common commitment to metaphysical speculation and robust ontological realism, 5; conceiving existence of things outside our own conceptions of them, 67; convergence between concerns of new materialism and, 5–11; differences among thinkers, 5, 10–11; dispute as to whether mathematics and science allow noncorrelational access to reality in, 119; epistemological thesis, 68; Harman's creative contribution to, 41; introduction of term, 5; new alternative from rise of, 27; ontological thesis, 68; original speculative realists, 65; paradoxical task of, 111, 113; questioning of anthropocentrism, 1, 8, 9; rejection of correlationism, 5–10, 63, 65, 66; revisions of Kantian settlement, 67, 69–75, 78, 138, 146, 148; risk taken by, 9–10; speculation as both subtractive and additive, 111; varieties of, 65, 68–69; Whitehead's place in genealogy of, 28. *See also* object-oriented ontology; panpsychism

of, 111–12. *See also* correlationism; mentality

time and space, apprehension of, 155

tool-being, 49–53; doubleness of, 50–53; doubleness of, as retreat and eruption, 51–53; as expansion of Heidegger's readiness-to-hand, Harman on, 49–51

Tool-Being (Harman), 50–51

tools: as actants, 48; Aleutian versus human, in Jones's "The Universe of Things," 46–48; readiness-to-hand, 48–49

Totality and Infinity (Levinas), 20–22; analysis of enjoyment in, 20–21; encounter with the Other and demands of ethical transcendence in, 21–22, 25

totalization, 69

Tractatus (Wittgenstein), 94

transcendence: demands of ethical, Levinas on, 21–22, 25; immanent place for, Whitehead on, 23–24

"Transcendental Aesthetic" (Kant), 155

transcendental argument, Kant's, 6–7, 28, 70, 71, 110

transcendental empiricism, 71–72

transcendental idealism, 71

transcendental realism, 71, 121–22

transfinites, Cantor's theory of, 69, 122

transition, as basis of continuity, 23

Trewavas, Anthony, 88, 126

Truth and Beauty, Whitehead on, 19–20, 41–42, 78

Tulving, Endel, 132

universality: of aesthetic judgment, 153; of cognitive or moral judgment, 152–53; conditions of, 150; singularity and, 149–54

"Universe of Things, The" (Jones), 45–49; assumption of mechanic in, 50; double movement of tool-being in, 51–52; human versus Aleutian technology in,

46–48; mechanic's experience of tools in, 47, 48, 52, 54, 59

univocity of being, Deleuze's doctrine of, 150

value: creativity as highest, Whitehead on, 4, 8; entities as autonomous centers of, 89–91; and fact, entwining of, 24–25, 26; responsibility and, 25; Whitehead's definition of, 89; Wittgenstein's claim of valuelessness, 77

Van der Tuin, Iris, 11

Varela, 144

vector transmission, process of, 28

vicarious affection, 70

vicarious causation, Harmon on, 33, 37, 56, 70, 118, 138, 146, 148, 151

vicarious sensation/enjoyment, 151, 152

vitalism, 62–63; dark, 83

vitalist materialism, 11, 48, 62; panexperientialism or panpsychism and, 63

Western philosophy: bifurcation of nature reinforced in, 3; correlationism dominating, 6, 7–8; dualisms of, 30, 58, 61, 62, 99, 153–54; grounded on idealization of human mind and rationality, 87; Whitehead's critique of, 25–26, 28

"What Is It Like to Be a Bat?" (Nagel), 91–92

Whitehead, Alfred North, 51; accusation of anthropomorphism against, 90–91; actualism of, 34–35, 37; aestheticized account of ethics, 24, 25–26; atomism of, 3, 23, 34–35, 104; on bifurcation of nature as basic error of modern Western thought, 114; on bipolarity of actual entity, 63; on blind emotion as primitive form of experience, 79–80; causal efficacy notion of, 55–60; on "chief error" of Western philosophy, 25–26; comparing Levinas with, 20–27; on consciousness, 79;

(continued from page ii)

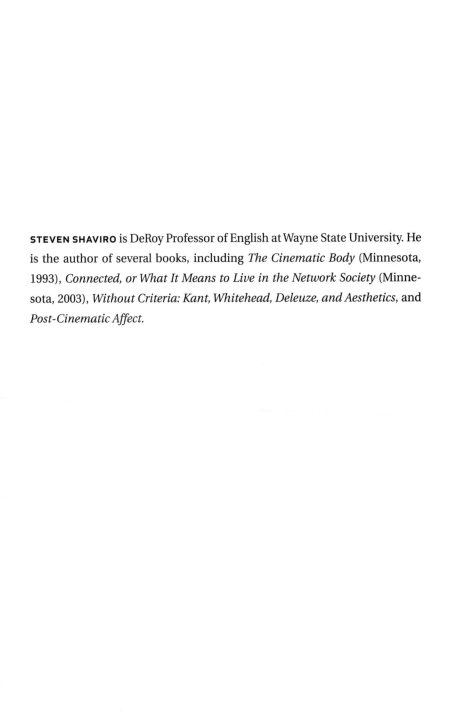
STEVEN SHAVIRO is DeRoy Professor of English at Wayne State University. He is the author of several books, including *The Cinematic Body* (Minnesota, 1993), *Connected, or What It Means to Live in the Network Society* (Minnesota, 2003), *Without Criteria: Kant, Whitehead, Deleuze, and Aesthetics*, and *Post-Cinematic Affect*.